Do-It-Yourself

MANDOLIN

BY JEREMY CHAPMAN

To access audio and video, visit:
www.halleonard.com/mylibrary

Enter Code
4755-2768-6435-1025

ISBN 978-1-70517-733-4

Visit Hal Leonard Online at
www.halleonard.com

World headquarters, contact:
Hal Leonard
7777 West Bluemound Road
Milwaukee, WI 53213
Email: info@halleonard.com

In Europe, contact:
Hal Leonard Europe Limited
Dettingen Way
Bury St Edmunds, Suffolk, IP33 3YB
Email: info@halleonardeurope.com

In Australia, contact:
Hal Leonard Australia Pty. Ltd.
4 Lentara Court
Cheltenham, Victoria, 3192 Australia
Email: info@halleonard.com.au

CONTENTS

INTRODUCTION

Do-It-Yourself Mandolin is intended to be a self-paced, self-teaching guide for learning how to play the mandolin. Though I feel there is nothing better than having a qualified, real-life teacher working with you one-on-one—offering instruction to help you avoid the pitfalls and providing feedback—private lessons aren't always an option. If you do have a teacher, this book can be used as a primer to help you get ready for your first in-person lesson.

In the following pages, I will offer up complete mandolin instruction from beginner to intermediate level in clear, easy-to-understand language. As is the case with learning any specialized skill, there will be a number of techniques that take time to internalize and master, as well as a new vocabulary of terms and phrases related to music in general, and to the mandolin specifically. But don't fret (a musical pun you'll soon get), you'll be speaking the new language and creating music before you know it.

Coming from a background of bluegrass and fiddle tunes, I personally think the best way to learn to play music is to just start playing. With that in mind, most new techniques will be introduced within a song, melody, or exercise. In fact, it's my goal for you to be playing your first song within a few minutes of reading this book. We'll start by getting a basic overview of the different parts of the mandolin, how to hold it and your pick, and a brief introduction to tablature and notation.

About the Audio/Video

Go to **www.halleonard.com/mylibrary** and enter the code found on page 1 of this book to access the accompanying audio and video files for download or streaming. Examples with accompanying media are marked with an audio or video icon as shown.

Chapter 1:
The Basics

In this chapter, we will develop a foundational understanding of the parts and language of the mandolin. We will discuss posture, proper pick grip, and how to tune your mandolin. You will also learn how to use tablature and start to develop the fundamental skills to begin making music.

Parts of the Mandolin

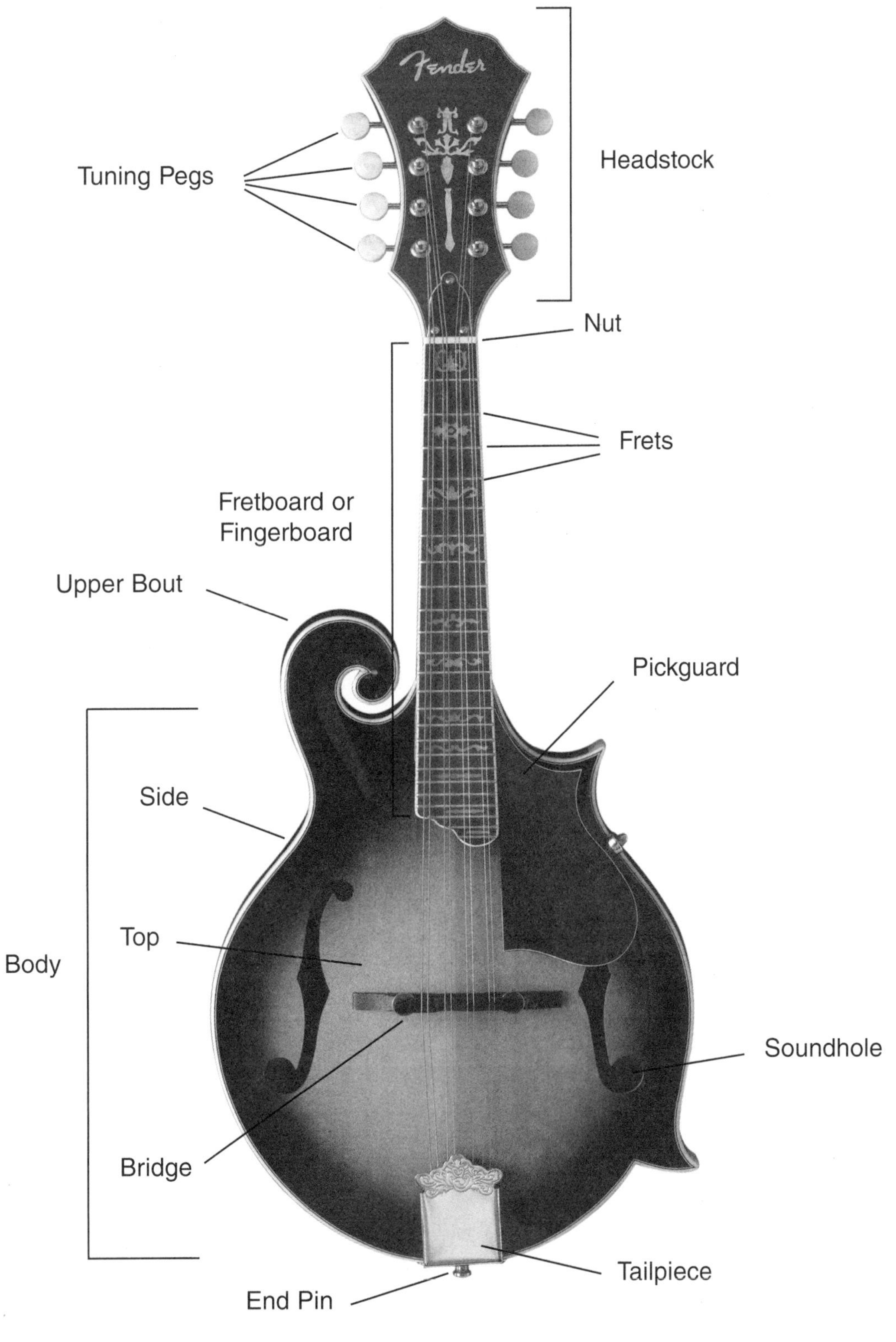

Though you could learn to play the mandolin without knowing the different parts that make up the instrument, it is best to know the "doohickey" from the "thingamabob." One of the great joys of music is the communal aspect of collaborating with other musicians, so it is very helpful to feel comfortable "speaking the language." It will also be helpful as I describe techniques in the following lessons. So let's start out with a basic diagram of the mandolin. If you want a further understanding of the different parts, check out the associated video.

Posture 

Just as there are widely accepted stances when taking a golf swing, there are "best practices" for holding a mandolin. There may always be a "John Daly" out there breaking the rules, but for the rest of us, here's what I have found will lead to the most success and the least strain on your body.

When sitting, keep a relaxed posture with the mandolin resting on your right thigh. If you have an "F" style mandolin, rest the bottom point of the instrument on the inside of your thigh for support. If using a strap, try setting your strap length when sitting so that your mandolin will be in the same relative position when standing.

Fingers of the Fret Hand

If you're right-handed, then typically your left hand will be your fret hand. The fingers of the fret hand are numbered 1–4. (**Note:** We don't use our thumb to press down the strings, so we don't assign it a number.)

Keep your palm away from the neck of the mandolin, almost as if you're holding a small ball between your palm and the neck. The points of contact are the first knuckle of your first finger on the bottom edge of the neck, and the second knuckle of your thumb on the top edge of the neck.

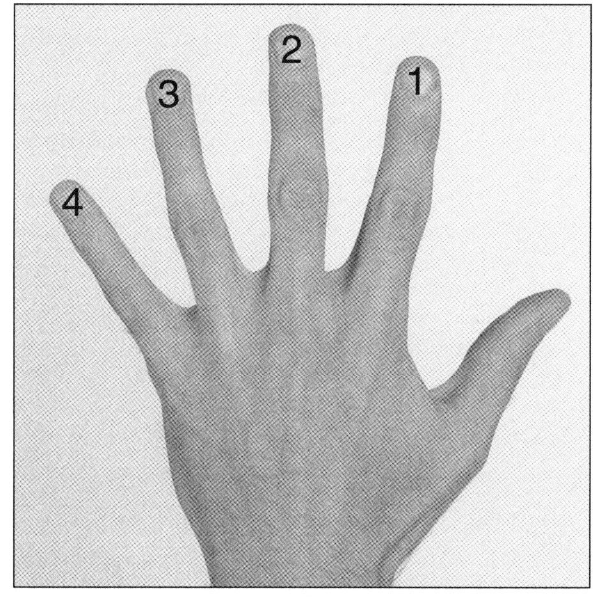

TOOLBOX

TIP: When fretting a note, place your finger directly behind the fret wire and try to bump right up against it to get the clearest note. If you do this, you shouldn't have to push down as hard either. Calluses will eventually form on your fingertips and will make this much easier in time. Even with the small space between frets on a mandolin, the difference in clarity between a note fretted at the back of the space between the frets versus bumped right up against the fret is huge.

Holding the Pick

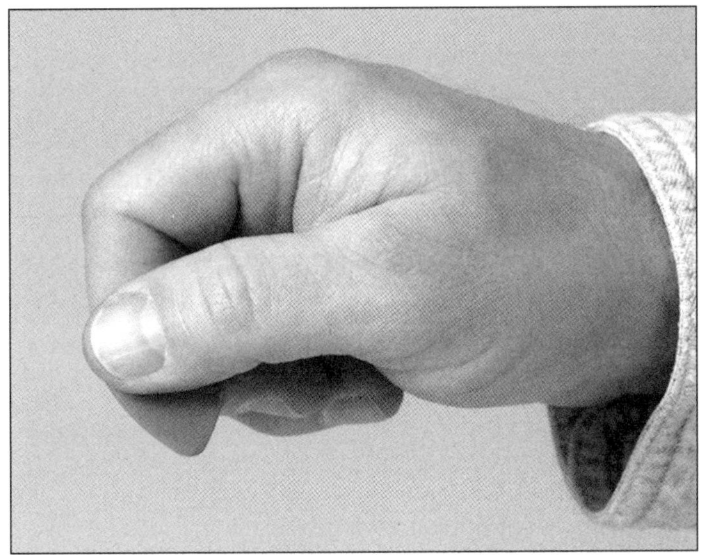

If you're right-handed, then typically your right hand will be your pick hand. Position your pick hand as if you're holding an invisible gun, with your middle, ring, and pinky fingers holding the grip, and your index finger at the trigger. Now bring your palm in front of your belly with your index finger pointing towards your navel. Place the flat pick on the *side* of your index (trigger) finger so that the point of it is facing the same direction as your fingertip. Lower your thumb over the pick to provide a gentle grip on the pick. You'll want to hold the pick as loosely as you can without dropping it. This is the most common pick grip, though by no means is it the only way. At first, you will feel the pick turning in your hand while playing. You might feel like you're about to drop the pick, and you may do so from time to time. Eventually, you'll develop a feel for just enough pressure to hold the pick, but no more.

Resting Your Pick Hand

To help control your pick hand, it is best to find an anchor point on the mandolin. When soloing, I recommend setting the heel of your palm (on the pinky side) down on the strings behind the bridge, right on the A and D strings. This point of contact becomes a pivot point, gaining more control over the pick and allowing the wrist to make fine-tuned motions over the strings. It also helps to create a muscle memory of the location of the different strings in space by setting a reference point for your hand. Note that when strumming rhythm, simply resting your forearm on the side of the mandolin, instead, allows for a full swing of your hand across all of the strings in a quick motion, while providing control of both your hand and the entire mandolin.

Tuning Your Mandolin

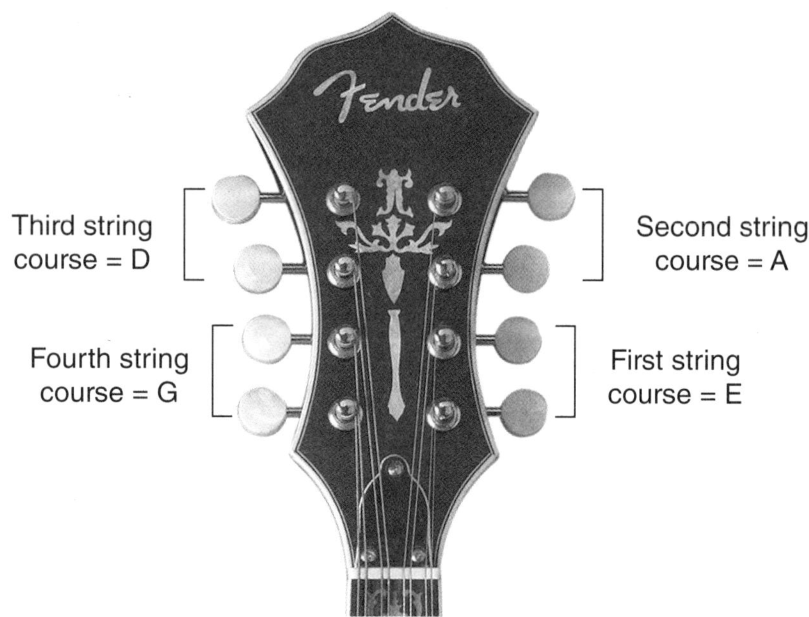

One of the unique things about the mandolin is that each string is doubled, so there are four *pairs* of strings (called *courses*), and therefore, eight total strings. Each pair is tuned to the same pitch. The overall tuning is the same as the violin: G-D-A-E, from lowest pitch to highest. We just double up each note with a second string, GG-DD-AA-EE.

Be sure to invest in an electronic tuner. Good quality "clip on" tuners are affordable. Because there are eight strings and tuning pegs, one of the most common early mistakes is turning the wrong tuning peg. The best way to avoid this is to start on the peg closest to you (low G) and work your way out, around, and back in on the bottom side (to high E). To start, trace the string from where you're plucking it with your pick all the way up to the tuning peg to confirm that it's the correct one. Always start with the low-pitched G string, as it has the highest tension and can pull on the neck, changing the pitch of the other strings. Watch the accompanying video for details on tuning the mandolin.

TOOLBOX

TIP: If you find yourself turning a tuning peg without seeing or hearing a change in pitch, trace the string from your pick hand up to the corresponding peg on the headstock to confirm that you're turning the correct one.

Reading Tablature

Tablature is like the "paint-by-numbers" way to read music. Standard notation requires learning how to read the pitch and length of the notes on the staff, and then learning where all the notes are located on your instrument. While this is a great skill to possess, it can delay the "playing music" part of your journey by quite a bit and can sometimes lead to giving up early. Fretted instrument players can use tablature (or "tab") to write out melodies and chords.

Each line of the tab represents a string of your instrument. (In our case, this is a pair of strings, or course, but we'll use the word "string" in this book to keep it simple.) Mandolin tab has four lines—one for each string. The most confusing part of tablature is that it looks upside down to how you hold your mandolin. This is in keeping with traditional notation by placing the lower-pitched notes at the bottom of the staff and the higher-pitched notes at the top. The low G line at the bottom of the staff corresponds to the big string closest to the ceiling (when you're holding the mandolin), while the high E line at the top of the staff represents the thin string closest to the floor.

Each fret on the mandolin is represented by its number on the corresponding string on the staff. For example, the number "2" placed on the top line tells you to play the note on the 2nd fret of the E string; "5" written on the third line down from the top would tell you to pick the D string with your fret-hand finger on the 5th fret. A "0" on a line means the string is to be played *open*, or without holding down any frets.

Let's try playing our first song using tablature. I love starting with this song because it begins with two open strings and is a melody so ingrained in our memories that we know what it is supposed to sound like, making learning it that much easier.

TWINKLE, TWINKLE LITTLE STAR

Traditional

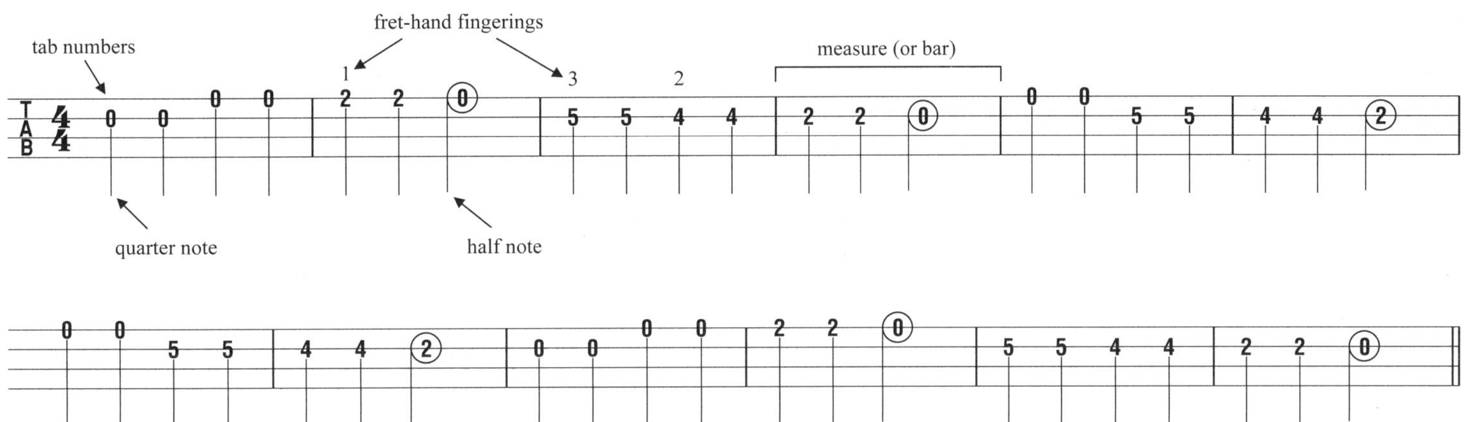

You're going to start with two zeros on the second line, telling you to play the open A string two times with no fret-hand fingers touching the strings. This is followed by two more open notes with the E string. Notice there are four total notes in the first "box," which is called a *measure* (or "bar"). These four notes are *quarter notes*. You can tell that they are quarter notes by the single lines, or *stems*, drawn down underneath their corresponding tab numbers. In this song example, each quarter note represents one beat, and there are four beats in each measure.

The second measure starts with "2 - 2" on the top line. This tells you to hold down the 2nd fret on the E string and play it twice. The small "1" floating above the staff is a fret-hand fingering, which instructs you to use the first finger of your fret hand to hold down the 2nd fret.

The "0" in the third beat position of the second measure again means you play the open E string. However, did you notice the circle around this note? It tells you this note is a *half note*, which is equal in value to two quarter notes, and therefore, lasts for two beats. Like quarter notes, a half note also has a stem, but it has the added circle as well. So when you pluck this half note, let it ring for two beats, which includes beats 3 and 4 of that measure, instead of one beat like the quarter notes. Just think of how you would sing this song; tap your finger with each syllable you sing: "Twin-kle, twin-kle, lit-tle star"... Notice how you hold the word "star" longer than the syllables of "twinkle" and "little."

Moving on, we have "55 44 22 0" on the A string. Remember, the number above the staff indicates which fret-hand finger to use. The general rule to follow is that each finger of your fret hand is responsible for two frets: the 1st and 2nd frets are fretted with your first (or index) finger, the 3rd and 4th frets with your second (or middle) finger, the 5th and 6th frets with your third (or ring) finger, and finally, your fourth (or pinky) finger will be used on the 7th fret. This configuration indicates what is called *first position* on the fretboard. As we change positions, finger indications will be written above the notes on the staff.

Continue playing the song as written in the tablature.

Congratulations! You've played your first song, or songs, as "Twinkle, Twinkle Little Star," "ABC Song," "Baa Baa Black Sheep," and "Johny Johny Yes Papa" all share the same melody.

Chapter 2: Fundamentals

There are a number of foundational skills to develop with our right and left hands to progress on the mandolin. The more time you can spend practicing these skills, the quicker and more consistently you'll improve with playing melodies and gaining speed.

Pick Stroke Theory

The pick hand is often the most overlooked in learning to play a fretted instrument. We often look to our fret hand to see where our fingers are landing on the fretboard, hoping that the pick is finding the same string that our finger lands on. Spending time training your pick hand will lead to much faster progress in the long run. There are two motions that we can make with the pick: down or up. I like to think of these two motions as our two legs, right and left. You can easily hop on one leg (right, right, right) at a slow steady pace, but if you want to run, you get both legs in on the action (right, left, right, left...). Now, if you were running at this fast pace and alternating between right and left, then suddenly took two right steps in a row, you would most likely stumble for a moment before recovering; the same is true for alternating between down and up with your pick. To help us get started, there are some general rules about which direction to use on a given beat.

We will get into counting rhythm more in the next section, but to start training your pick hand, there are two basic options. If there is just a single vertical line, or stem, under a note (tab number on the staff), that note is a quarter note and will always be played with a downstroke of your pick: 1, 2, 3, 4 = down, down, down, down. This is indicated in tab with the following symbol: ⊓. An upstroke with your pick is indicated with this symbol: V.

If two or more note stems are beamed together, the first note is a downstroke, the second note is an upstroke, etc. The upstroke is on the "and" count, between the numbers, while the downstroke is on the numbered count. "1/and, 2/and, 3/and, 4/and" would be played: down/up, down/up, down/up, down/up. The following exercises are some "tongue twisters" for your pick hand. They're great to help internalize the alternating picking pattern as well as to map out in space the distance between the strings.

TOOLBOX

Repeats

In the following exercises, notice the vertical bars with dots on both ends of the staff. These are called *repeats* (or *repeat bars*), and they tell you to repeat everything in between them. So, after you play through the music once, return back to the beginning without pausing and continue playing through the whole exercise again. For these types of exercises, you can keep repeating them in a loop as long as you'd like, as they are designed for practicing.

Notice that the notes in the first exercise have stems that are beamed together. These types of notes are called *eighth notes*, and each one lasts for half the duration of a quarter note. For this exercise, you will play four eighth notes on each string from low (pitch) to high, and then work back down to the low string. Since the notes are beamed together, you will alternate between downstrokes and upstrokes. Focus on your pick hand, and make sure you keep it planted behind the bridge. Double-check that your pick grip is relaxed but controlled. Are you hitting both pairs of strings on both the downstrokes and upstrokes? Is the time between notes evenly spaced?

Pick-Hand Exercise 1

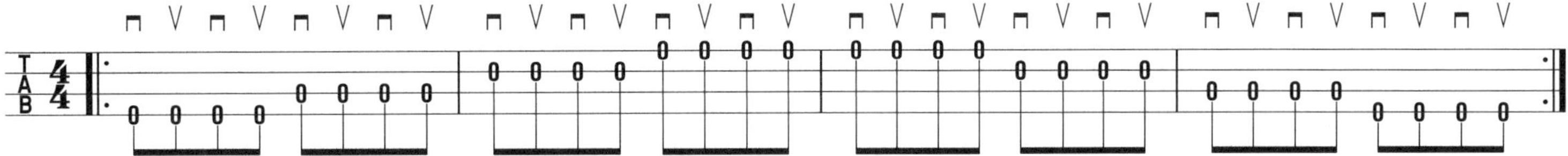

In the next exercise, we'll alternate between the D and A strings. The first measure starts on the D string with the downstroke on the *downbeat* (the counted beat), and then the A string is picked on the "and" count, or *upbeat*, and played with an upstroke. Pick down on the D string, move the pick past the A string to catch it on an upstroke, then past the D string to catch it on a downstroke, etc. The second measure flips the pattern by starting on the A string for the downbeat downstroke, then catching the D string with an upstroke, etc.

Pick-Hand Exercise 2

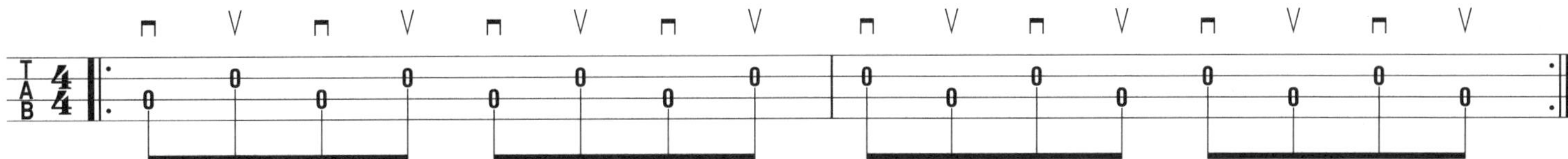

The third exercise will help to map the distance between the G string and each of the others, as well as train you to go past the next string to catch it on an upstroke. You will pass the D string on the "and" count to catch it on an upstroke, then pass the G string to start with a downstroke on the second set.

Pick-Hand Exercise 3

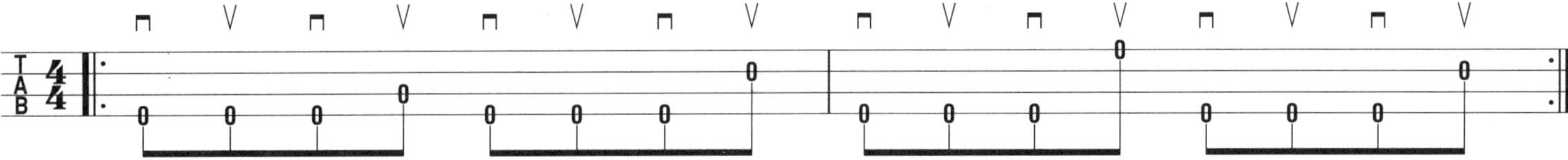

The fourth exercise complicates things by changing the alternating note to every third note. It helps at first to break it into three-note packets. Since we play the A string with a downstroke the first time through the pattern, the next packet of the same three notes has to start with an upstroke on the E string, the next with a downstroke, and so on.

Pick-Hand Exercise 4

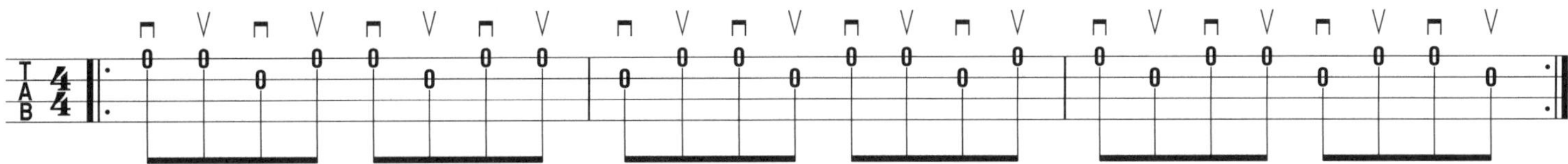

Once you feel comfortable and proficient with the fourth exercise, move on to this final exercise, which alternates between playing every third note on the A, D, and G strings.

Pick-Hand Exercise 5

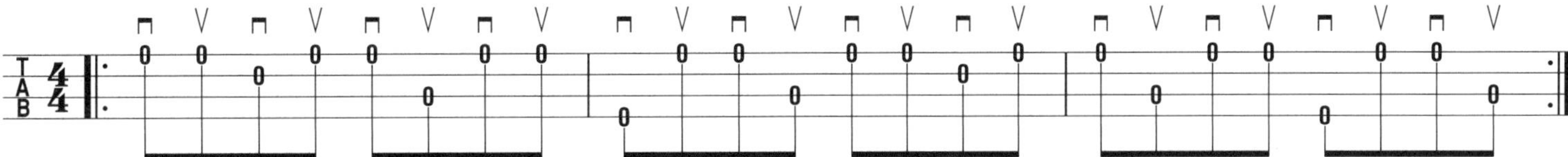

Scales and Patterns

We'll not attempt to learn scales for every key or all the different patterns you can play them in, but instead, I'll share some that I have found most useful in playing melodies. As you may recall from the songs of *The Sound of Music*, we use scales to create melodies. They represent the distance between notes that "sound good" together. Using the basic *major scale* pattern, you can play most of the melodies you're familiar with in Western music. The distance between notes or intervals in the major scale follows the same pattern: two whole steps, one half step, three whole steps, and one half step... or, whole-whole-half-whole-whole-whole-half.

We can play a G major scale by starting on the G note, moving two frets (or one whole step) up to the A note, two more frets to the B note, one fret (or one half step) to the C note, two frets to the D note, two frets to the E note, two frets to the F♯, and one last fret to the G note that is one *octave* (or eight notes) higher than the starting G note. This is the familiar "do, re, mi, fa, sol, la, ti, do." Let's try this on the mandolin.

Starting by playing the open G string, we then play our first two whole steps with the 2nd and 4th frets, then our first half step with the 5th fret. Another whole step would take us to the 7th fret, which on the mandolin is the same note as the next higher open string; so instead, we'll play the open D string and continue with two more whole steps. The final half step is the octave G note at the 5th fret. Now play the scale backwards from the high G on the 5th fret of the D string back down to the low open G string. (For a deeper dive into music theory, check out *Music Theory: A Practical Guide for All Musicians*, available from Hal Leonard.)

One-Octave Quarter-Note G Scale

In the previous example, each note of the G scale was equal to a quarter note and played with downstrokes only. Let's play the same exact scale but change each note into eighth notes, alternating our pick direction.

One-Octave Eighth-Note G Scale

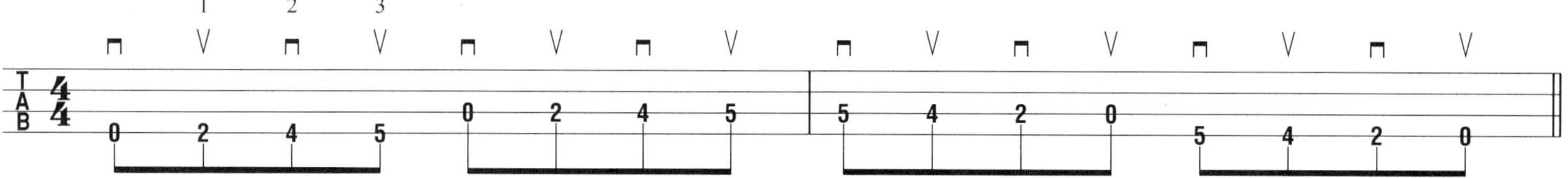

As you can see, we now have one octave fitting into each measure. The note stems are beamed together indicating they are eighth notes, so we start each grouping with a downstroke and end with an upstroke. Let's try a two-octave G scale with eighth-note values.

Two-Octave Eighth-Note G Scale

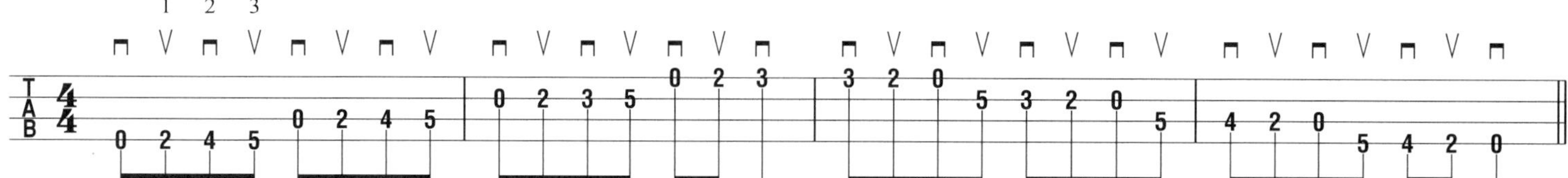

Counting Beats

Along with the different notes that we use to make music, we also vary the length of the notes to create a melody. You can think of it much like a ruler. Each inch mark on the ruler is like a measure on the staff. Just as each inch can be divided into 1/2", 1/4", 1/8", 1/16", so can each measure of music by using different note lengths: 1 full measure, 1/2 measure, 1/4 measure, 1/8 measure, 1/16 measure. Respectively, we name these note types like this: whole note (1 measure), half note (1/2 measure), quarter note (1/4 measure), eighth note (1/8 measure), and sixteenth note (1/16 measure). Instead of measuring the physical length of things like a ruler, they measure the length of time passing—how long a note rings out, or the empty space between. The number of beats you need to count for each of these different types of notes is shown in the following table.

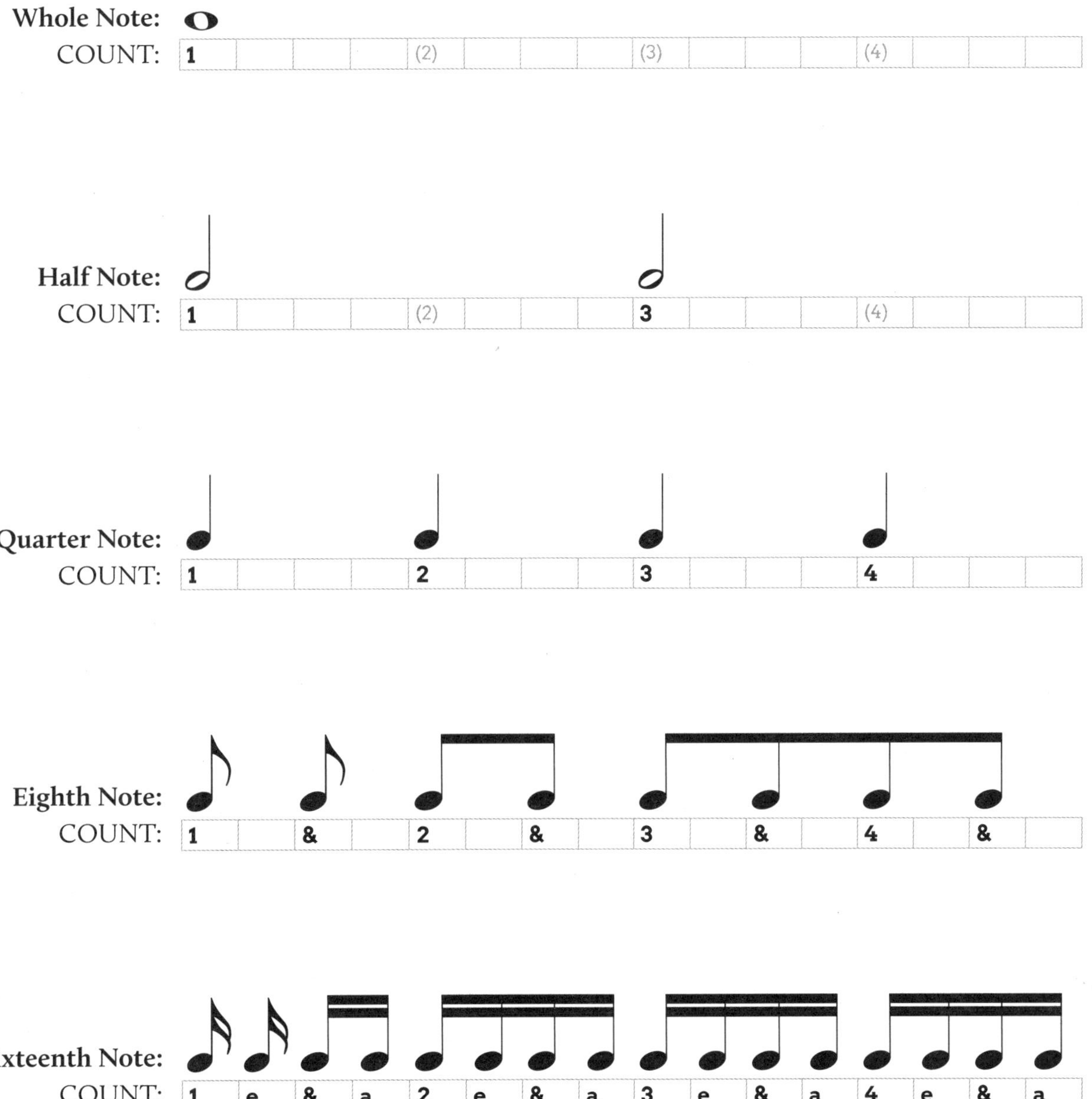

When we played "Twinkle, Twinkle Little Star," each note lasted one-quarter of each measure, and hence, they were quarter notes. We can play the same melody with each note lasting an eighth of a measure by using eighth notes. With the eighth notes, we will alternate our pick stroke by counting "1 and, 2 and, 3 and, 4 and" for each measure. All of the numbered counts are the downbeats, while the "and" counts are upbeats.

TWINKLE, TWINKLE LITTLE STAR

Eighth Notes

Traditional

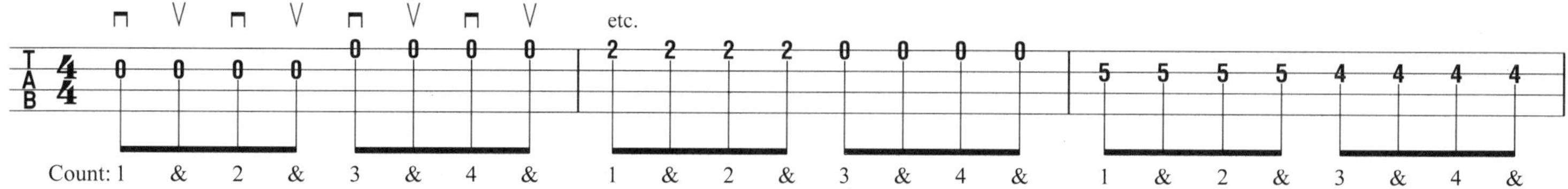

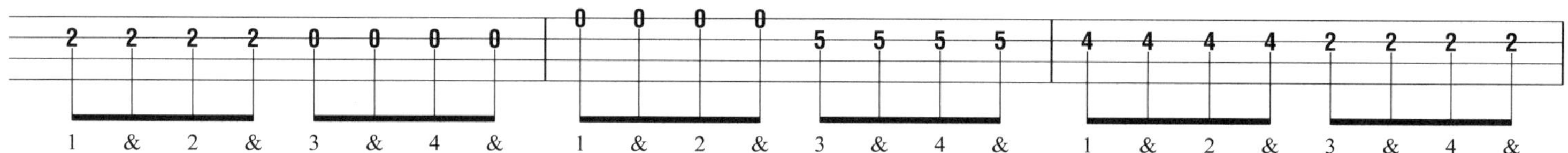

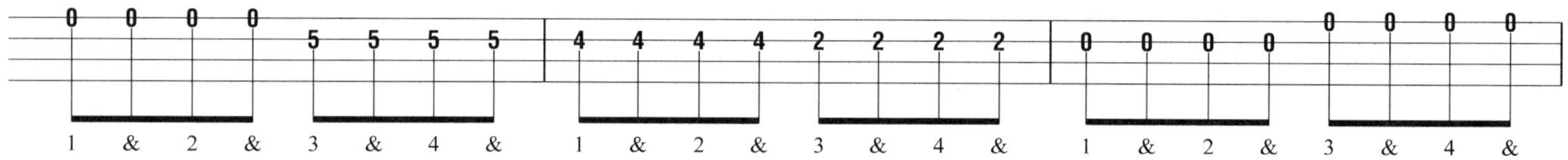

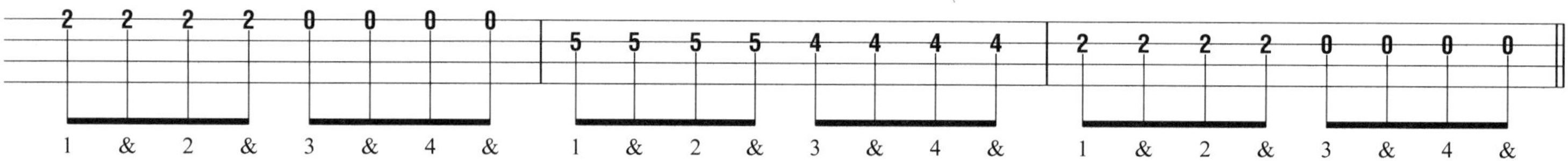

With all of the notes the same length, we start to lose some of the "feel" of the melody. It sounds like "Twinkle, Twinkle Little Star," but not quite right. We can mix both quarter notes and eighth notes to create a more interesting melody than the all-quarter-note version, but less overwhelming than the all-eighth-note version.

In this next version, each measure is divided into one quarter note and two eighth notes followed by two more quarter notes. We count it as "1, 2 and, 3, 4" and we pick it down, down-up, down, down. Just like a ruler evenly divides 1/2", 1/4", etc., the eighth notes should be exactly half as long as the quarter notes. The "and" count should be evenly spaced right between the 2 and 3 counts.

TWINKLE, TWINKLE LITTLE STAR

Mixed Notes

Traditional

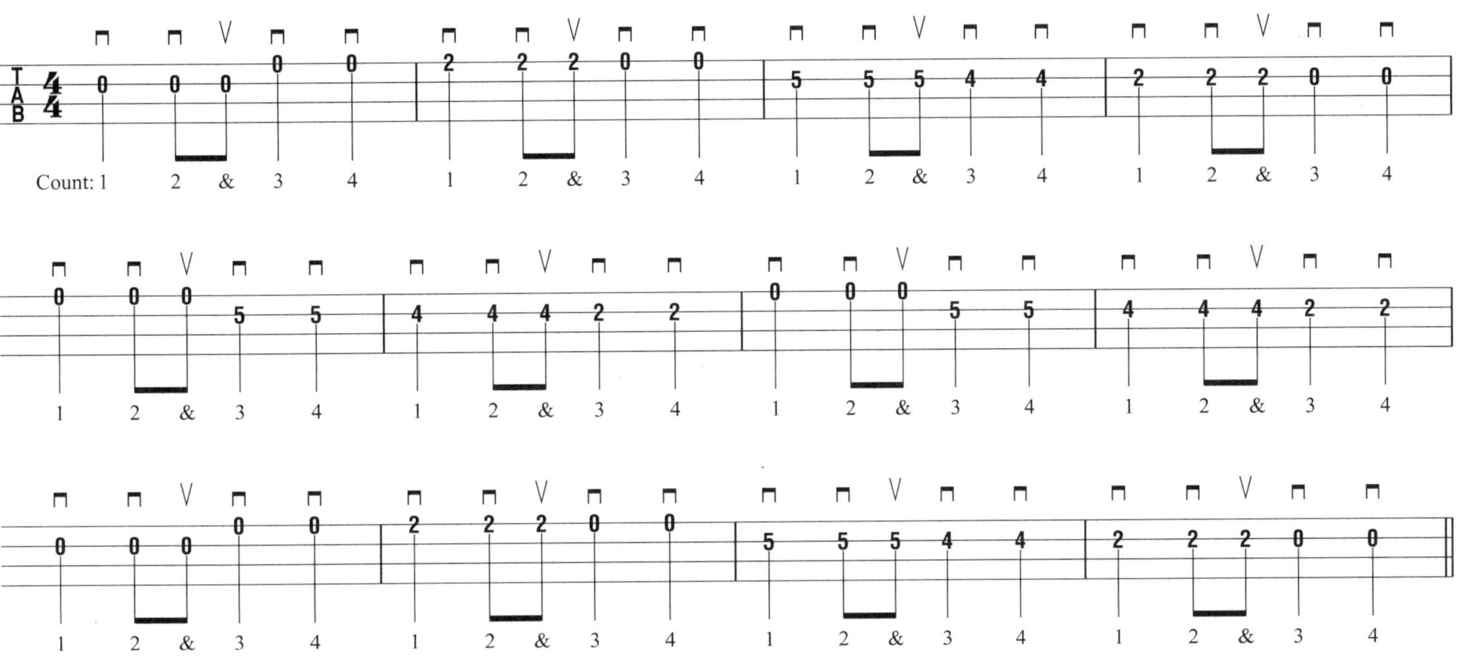

Let's try another familiar song, "Mary Had a Little Lamb." We'll start again with a quarter-note version that follows the syllables of the lyrics. Each syllable is a quarter note in length. Just like in our first version of "Twinkle, Twinkle Little Star," there are also half notes here starting on the third beat of several measures. There is also a new note type in the final measure of the tune: the *whole note*. A whole note has a circle around the tab number and no stem. It lasts for four beats, so let it ring for the entire measure.

MARY HAD A LITTLE LAMB

Words by Sarah Josepha Hale

Traditional Music

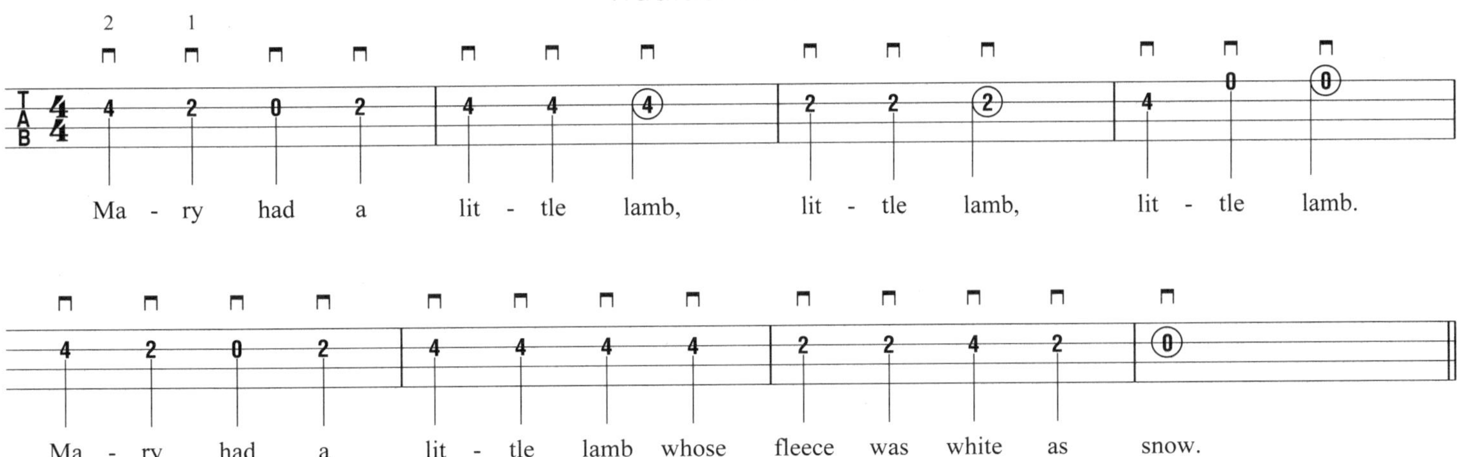

TOOLBOX

TIP: Try handing off each note to the next. What I mean by this is: unless a note is an open string (0), always keep the string pressed down until the next note. In the first measure of the following song, place your first finger on the 2nd fret before removing your second finger from the 4th fret; then, after playing the open string, hold down the 2nd fret at the end of the measure all the way until you add the second finger on the 4th fret to start the next measure. This lets the notes sustain into each other, sounding connected and more musical than if you had just stopped each note from ringing before the next one was played. Again, think how you would sing it: "Ma-ry had a lit-tle lamb," instead of "Ma. ry. had. a. lit. tle. lamb."

Now let's turn every other note into an eighth note, counted as "1, 2 and, 3, 4 and." Likewise, you'll pick down, down-up, down, down-up.

MARY HAD A LITTLE LAMB

Mixed Notes

Words by Sarah Josepha Hale
Traditional Music

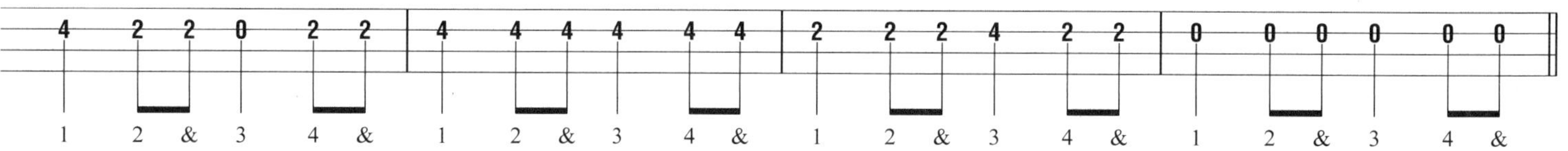

While you're getting familiar with the basics of counting rhythm, we'll stick to standard time, or *4/4 meter*, as it is the most common in Western music. The two "4's" stacked on top of each other at the beginning of the pieces we've looked at is called a *time signature*; it tells you that there are four beats per measure and each beat is equivalent to one quarter note in length. Later in the book, we'll learn about other time signatures that you'll run across and how to interpret them.

Chapter 3: Backup Rhythm & Chords

So far, we have talked about rhythm in the sense of playing a melody. We also count rhythm when accompanying other musicians—we play "backup" or "rhythm" chords while others are playing the melody on their instruments or singing. This is where the mandolin fills a unique role by playing on the "off" beats, or on beats 2 and 4 of the measure. An easy way to think about it is by imagining a two-piece drum set. The kick drum plays on beats 1 and 3 of the measure, and the snare drum on beats 2 and 4 (1, 2, 3, 4 = Kick, Snare, Kick, Snare). In a band, usually the bass instrument is playing the role of the kick drum and the mandolin is the snare.

You can try this with your mandolin. Tap your foot down like a kick drum and count "1," lift it up and count "2," down again "3," up "4." Do this for a while until you achieve an even space between each count. Then on the 2 and 4 counts, when your foot goes up, strum down on the strings of your mandolin: 1-strum-3-strum. Your hand and foot will be going in opposite directions: when your foot taps down, your hand goes up, and when your foot goes up, your hand strums down.

Learning to play backup rhythm is very important if you want to play with other musicians. Even the most skilled lead instrumentalists spend most of the time playing rhythm when others are involved. If someone is singing or playing the melody, our job is to help keep the rhythm of the song steady and support the melody by playing the correct chord changes.

Chords

There are two common ways to play chords on the mandolin, *barre chords* and *bluegrass "chop" chords*. Depending on the style of music you're playing, you may prefer one over the other, but it's recommended to be proficient at both. Once you've learned some of the common barre chord shapes, any of them can simply be moved around the neck to play every chord available without needing to learn and memorize every possible chord. We'll start with the "open" versions of the bluegrass chop chords, which include open strings and some fretted notes.

The best way to illustrate how to form a chord is by using a *chord frame*. Let's go over how to read one, using the following chord frame. The chord frame's vertical lines represent the mandolin's four string courses, as if you stood it up with the strings facing you. The low G string is on the left side, and the high E string is on the right. The horizontal lines represent the frets, with the thick line at the top indicating the nut. Placing an "O" above the nut tells us that the string it's placed above is played open, whereas an "X" above the string means it is not played or is muted. A dot on a string indicates a fretted note, telling you exactly where on the fretboard to press down. The numbers at the bottom tell you which fret-hand finger to use on that fret.

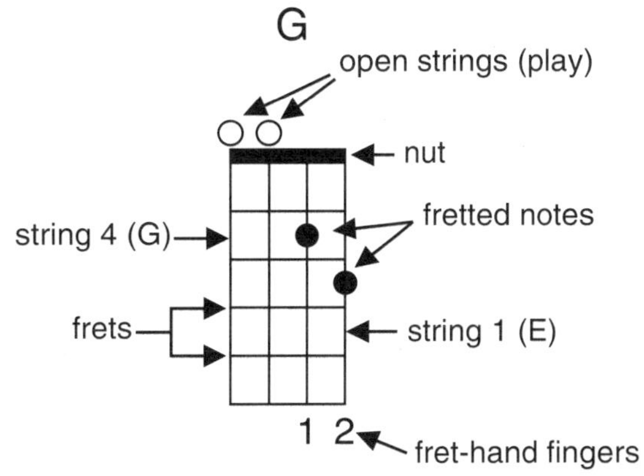

The first chord we're learning, shown in the previous frame, is a two-finger G chord. As indicated in the chord frame, the G and D strings are played open. Your first finger will be on the 2nd fret of the A string, and your second finger will be on the 3rd fret of the E string. Try strumming the chord, brushing your pick down across all four strings. Do each of the notes ring clearly? Most likely the open G and D strings are clear. Make sure that your first and second fingers are bumped right up against the frets. Also make sure that the second finger isn't touching the A string, muting it or changing its pitch. Try playing each string one at a time to hear if they are all ringing clearly.

Now we're going to strum the G chord on every beat for four measures. When strumming chords, keep your pick hand lifted off of the "solo" planting position behind the bridge, so your wrist and hand are generally loose and able to strum across all four strings, but keep your forearm anchored to the side of the mandolin. Using all downstrokes, play the G chord on each beat count (1-2-3-4) for four measures; each slash mark in the music (four per measure) represents a beat. Try to keep the space between each strum evenly spaced.

G Chord Strumming Pattern

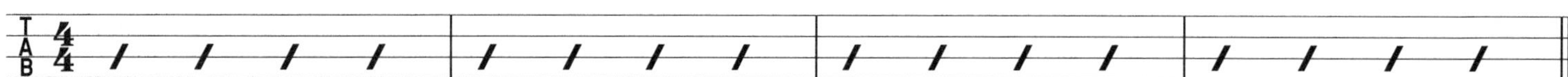

Next, let's learn the C chord. All we need to do is jump our fingering from the G chord over one string. As you can see in the chord frame, we have an open G string, a first finger on the 2nd fret of the D string, a second finger on the 3rd fret of the A string, and the open E string.

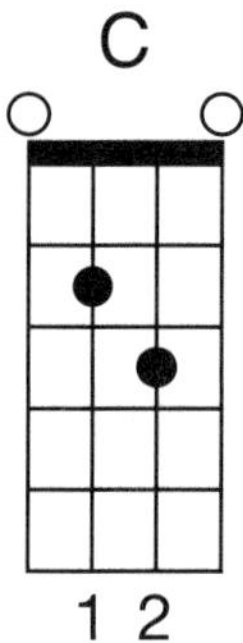

Now play the C chord on each downbeat for four measures.

C Chord Strumming Pattern

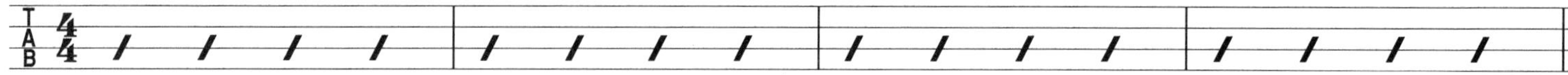

Even with the G and C chord shapes being virtually the same (just changing strings) it takes practice to get from one chord to the other in time. One of the best ways to practice this is to strum once on the first beat of each measure, then give yourself three beats to get to the next chord, strumming on the first beat of the next measure without delay.

G/C Chord Strumming Pattern 1

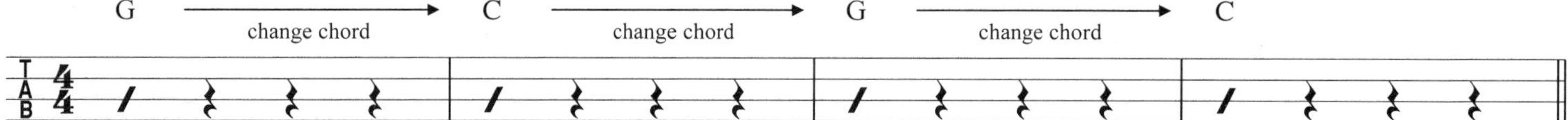

TOOLBOX

Rests

In the previous pattern, the symbol shown on beats 2, 3, and 4 in each measure is called a *rest*. Just like notes tell you to play for a certain duration, rests tell you to stop playing for a certain amount of time. The rests in music can be just as important as the notes. In this example, the rest used is called a *quarter rest*, and just like its counterpart the quarter note, it lasts for one full beat. Normally, you would need to stop the strings from ringing completely to properly observe a rest, however, for our purposes here of learning how to change chords, you can allow the strings to ring through as needed.

Once you are able to switch the chords back and forth in time, let's try switching to the off beats as discussed earlier. We'll play each chord on beats 2 and 4, while switching to the next chord on beat 1. (**Note**: The chord symbols have been placed over the off beats in this exercise for clarity, but usually in music chord symbols are placed where the chord change itself actually occurs, often over beat 1 or 3; when the mandolin is playing on the off beats, you won't play a chord right away when you see a chord symbol placed above beat 1 or 3.)

G/C Chord Strumming Pattern 2

Chop Chords

To create a more percussive sound on beats 2 and 4, or a "chop rhythm," *damping* is used. Damping involves cutting the sustain of the notes short by keeping your fingertips in contact with the strings, but not pressing down against the frets. It takes some coordination between your two hands to press the fingers of your fret hand down on the strings to make contact with the frets right before your pick hand strums with the pick, and then immediately let off the pressure of your fret-hand fingers to stop the strings from vibrating. You don't want to lift your fingers away from the strings; just let the tension of the strings lift your fingers away from the fretboard. It's the tips of your fingers making contact with the strings that damps or stops them from vibrating. This is where "chopping" gets its name—it's like the quick, dull sound of chopping wood. Though you can damp two-finger chords that have open strings by quickly slapping down your third and fourth fingers to stop all the strings from ringing, it's easiest at first to just pick the two strings that have fingers on them.

Here are the two-finger chop chords for the G and C chords you've already learned. The only difference is that you are only strumming the two fretted strings, and not the open strings (indicated by the "X").

Time to Play

Now that you are able to switch freely between the G and C chords, it's time to see how they fit together to create the foundation of music. There are quite a number of popular songs that can be played with just these two chords. In the following pages, I'll write out the lyrics to the songs along with the chord names written above. I've indicated where the 2 and 4 beats are with the placement of the chord names and slashes. Keep playing the same chord when you see a slash until a change to a new chord is indicated. Try playing both the open sustained chords and the "closed" chop chords. Listen to the examples to hear how each style sounds. Let's try a few popular songs.

MARY HAD A LITTLE LAMB

Chords

Words by Sarah Josepha Hale
Traditional Music

C / / / G / C /
Mary had a little lamb, little lamb, little lamb.

C / / / G / C /
Mary had a little lamb whose fleece was white as snow.

HE'S GOT THE WHOLE WORLD IN HIS HANDS

Traditional Spiritual

C / /
He's got the whole world in his hands.

C G / /
He's got the whole world in his hands.

G C / /
He's got the whole world in his hands.

C / G C /
He's got the whole world in his hands.

SKIP TO MY LOU

Traditional

C / / /
Skip, skip, skip to my Lou.

G / / /
Skip, skip, skip to my Lou.

C / / /
Skip, skip, skip to my Lou.

G / C /
Skip to my Lou, my darling.

YELLOW SUBMARINE

Words and Music by John Lennon and Paul McCartney

```
  C    /        G          /       /          /     C       /
We all live in a yellow submarine,  yellow submarine,  yellow submarine.
  C    /        G          /       /          /     C       /
We all live in a yellow submarine,  yellow submarine,  yellow submarine.
```


SHADY GROVE

Appalachian Folk Song

```
   C         /   /       /   /        /   /   /
Shady grove,  my little miss  Shady grove, my darlin'.
   C         /   /         /      G    /   C   /
Shady grove,  my little miss, I'm going  back to Harlan.
```


HOT CORN, COLD CORN

Traditional

```
   C         /         /           /
Hot corn, cold corn, bring along the demijohn.
   G         /         /           /
Hot corn, cold corn, bring along the demijohn.
   C         /         /           /
Hot corn, cold corn, bring along the demijohn.
       G          /          /          /     /     C   /   /
Fare thee well, Uncle Bill, see you in the morning, yes  sir.
```

I'M GOIN' BACK TO OLD KENTUCKY

Words and Music by Bill Monroe

```
              C  /    /    /    /    /   /
I'm going back _______ to old Kentucky, _______
      C      /   /   /    /     G    /   /
There to see _______ my Linda Lou. __________
   G          C  /    /    /    /    /   /
I'm going back _______ to old Kentucky, _______
        C       /  /  G     /      C   /   /
Where the skies _______ are always blue. __________
```


IT AIN'T GONNA RAIN NO MORE

Words and Music by Wendall Hall

```
      C           /        /       /
It ain't gonna rain no more, no more.
      C          /        G        /
It ain't gonna rain no more.
    G           /         /        /
How in the heck can I wash my neck if
      G          /       C         /
It ain't gonna rain no more?
```


TAKE ME BACK TO TULSA

Words by Tommy Duncan
Music by Bob Wills

```
     C        /   /   /       /         /    G   /
Take me back to Tulsa, _____ I'm too young to marry.
     G        /   /   /       /         /    C   /   /
Take me back to Tulsa, _____ I'm too young to marry.
```

Chapter 4:
The 1-4-5 Chord Progression

The most popular chord progression in Western music is called the "1-4-5" progression, sometimes presented as Roman numerals: I–IV–V. Countless songs, especially in folk and bluegrass, use just these three chords. So, what does it mean?

Whatever key you're playing a song in would be the "1" chord. So, let's say we're playing in the key of C as in the previous song; in this case, C is our "1" chord. Then, we just count up the alphabet starting from C to the fourth letter: C/1, D/2, E/3, **F**/4. F is our "4" chord. The next letter up from there is number 5, which makes G the "5" chord. Our 1, 4, and 5 chords in the key of C are C, F, and G. Let's move to the key of A and find the 1, 4, 5 there: **A**/1, B/2, C/3, **D**/4, **E**/5. So, our 1, 4, and 5 chords in the key of A are A, D, and E.

TOOLBOX

Keys

The term *key* in music refers to the *root note* or *tonic* that the melody is centered around. It will be the starting and ending note of the scale used to build the melody and the 1 chord that the chord progression is based upon. Though many melodies might not start on the root note, almost all of them will end on or resolve to the root.

For instance, "Mary Had a Little Lamb" started on the third note of the A scale (4th fret of the A string) when we played it earlier, but ended on the open A string, indicating that we played the melody in the key of A. If you were to play the same exact melody, but you started the pattern on the 4th fret of the D string instead, the final note would be an open D string, indicating the key of D.

In the chord sheet for "Mary Had a Little Lamb," C was our 1 chord and G was our 5 chord: **C**/1, D/2, E/3, F/4, **G**/5. If we wanted to play the chords in the key of A, then A would become our 1 chord and E our 5 chord: **A**/1, B/2, C/3, D/4, **E**/5.

In all of the two-chord songs played earlier, we were playing the 1 and 5 chords in the key of C. If we add the 4 chord, F, we can play thousands of songs. The great thing about the way the mandolin is tuned is that we can use the same chord shape we used previously and just change strings this time to the G and D strings.

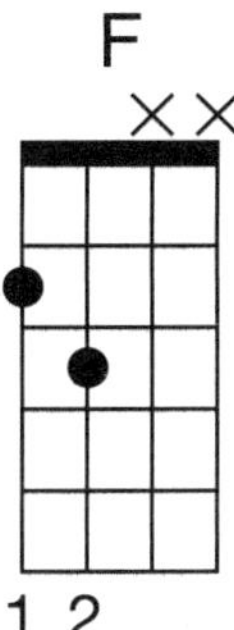

Let's try out the new F chord in some popular songs that use the 1, 4, and 5 chords in the key of C.

RING OF FIRE

Words and Music by Merle Kilgore and June Carter

G / / / F / C / G /
I fell into a burning ring of fire. I went down, down,

G / F / C / / /
down, and the flames went higher. And it burns, burns,

C / / F C / / G C /
burns, ______ that ring of fire, ______ that ring of fire.

KING OF THE ROAD

Words and Music by Roger Miller

C / F / G / C /
Trailers for sale or rent. Rooms to let, 50 cents.

C / F / G / / /
No phone, no pool, no pets. I ain't got no cigarettes.

C / F / G /
Two hours of pushin' brooms, buys an eight-by-twelve

C / / / F /
Four-bit room. I'm a man of means by no means,

G / C
King of the road.

MAN OF CONSTANT SORROW

Traditional

G / / / C / / /
In constant sorrow, all through his days. __________

C / / / / / / / F / /
I ______ am a man ______ of constant sorrow. ______

F G / / / C / / /
I've seen trou - ble all my day. __________

C / / / / / / / F /
I ______ bid farewell to old Kentucky,

F / G / / / C /
The place where I _____ was born and raised,

C / G / / / C / /
The place where I _____ was born and raised.

I SAW THE LIGHT

Words and Music by Hank Williams

```
      C    /     /    /      /   /          / /
I wandered so aimless,       life filled with sin.
 F    /      /      /       /  /   C  /
I wouldn't let      my     dear Savior in.
      C /          /        /        /    /          /  /
Then Jesus came       like      a stranger in the night.
    C /      /  /  G   /    C   /  /  /
Praise the Lord,      I saw the light.
```

Chorus

```
 C   /     /   /   /   /     /  /
I saw the light,      I saw the light.
   F  /   /   /   /  /   C  /
No more darkness, no more night.
     C /     /  /    /  /       /  /
Now I'm so happy, no sorrow in sight.
    C /      /  /  G   /    C   /  /  /
Praise the Lord,      I saw the light.
```


TOOLBOX

Finding the 1-4-5 Chords

Watch the accompanying video to learn about an easy way to find the three chords that make up the 1-4-5 pattern by following an L-shaped pattern on the fretboard. For instance, if you're playing in the key of G, then G will be the 1 chord, played on the 2nd and 3rd frets of the A and E strings, C is the 4 chord right above it on the 2nd and 3rd frets of the D and A strings (short part of the L-shape), and two frets forward from here on the 4th and 5th frets of the same strings is D, the 5 chord (long part of the L-shape).

In the key of A, the 4th and 5th frets of the A and E strings make the 1 chord (A), 4th and 5th frets of the D and A strings make the 4 chord (D), and 6th and 7th frets make the 5 chord (E). When playing in a key where your middle finger is on the A string, like the key of D, the L-shaped pattern is lying the other way. The 1 chord (D) is on the 4th and 5th frets of the D and A strings, down and back (long part of the L-shape) is the 4 chord (G) on the 2nd and 3rd frets of the A and E strings, and two frets higher to the 4th and 5th frets is the 5 chord (A).

Chapter 5:
Learning to Play Melodies

So far, we've learned how to play the melodies to "Twinkle, Twinkle Little Star" and "Mary Had a Little Lamb." A great next step is to learn some fiddle tunes, and there are hundreds of commonly played fiddle tunes that used to be performed at barn dances and on front porches across the United States.

A tradition with fiddle tunes is to first learn the basic melody, and then to build or embellish upon it with "runs" or "licks" for variation. In the following examples, I'll start with the fundamental melody, and then build or embellish on it by changing the rhythm or adding some runs between parts to give you an idea of how this practice works. Watch the accompanying video to see how we can do this with our next tune, "Boil Them Cabbage Down." (**Note**: You can come back and play the grayed-out chords shown throughout the book later, after you've learned more chords and comping patterns.)

BOIL THEM CABBAGE DOWN

Basic Melody

American Folksong

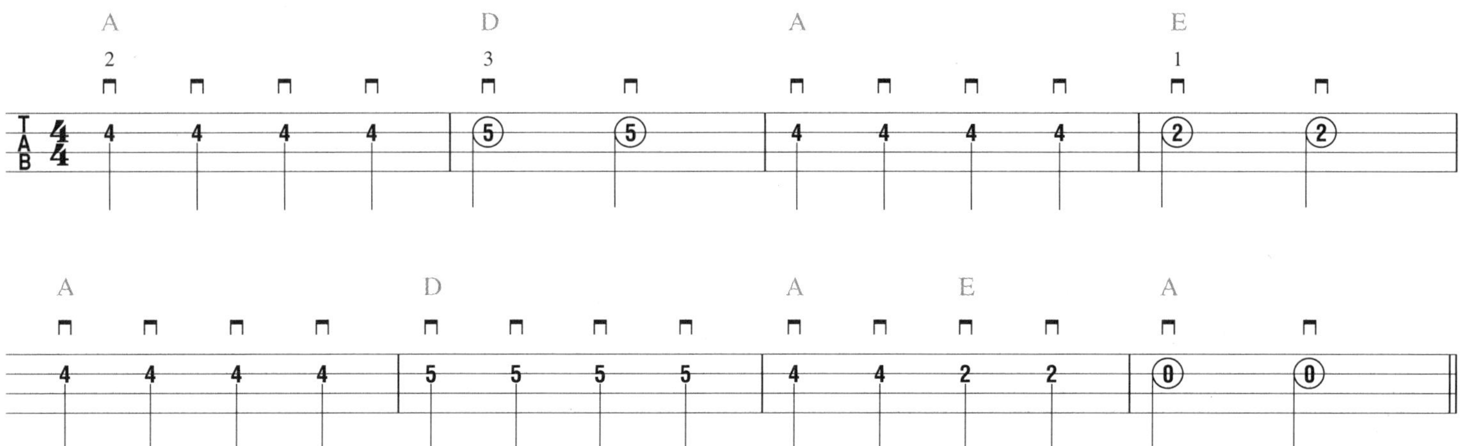

TOOLBOX

"Lick" or "Run" Defined

The term *lick*, or *run*, is applied to a series of notes that can be used, moved, and adjusted to fit in other iterations and melodies. They are like a phrase that we can memorize and place in other musical sentences or melodies. Just as we can connect a few words into a phrase and then insert this phrase into different places in conversation, a lick can be fit into different songs and melodies. For instance, the phrase "if I were you, I would" can be used at the beginning of a sentence: "If I were you, I would focus on pick-hand technique first." It can also be placed in the middle: "I'm not telling you what to do, but if I were you, I would practice three hours a day." Alternatively, it can be placed at the end: "You may decide to go ahead with banjo lessons, but I wouldn't if I were you."

We can borrow the shuffle pattern we used earlier in "Mary Had a Little Lamb" and build upon this basic melody by turning the quarter note on every second and fourth beat into two eighth notes. Remember to use upstrokes on the eighth notes that fall on the "and" counts.

BOIL THEM CABBAGE DOWN

Shuffle Pattern

American Folksong

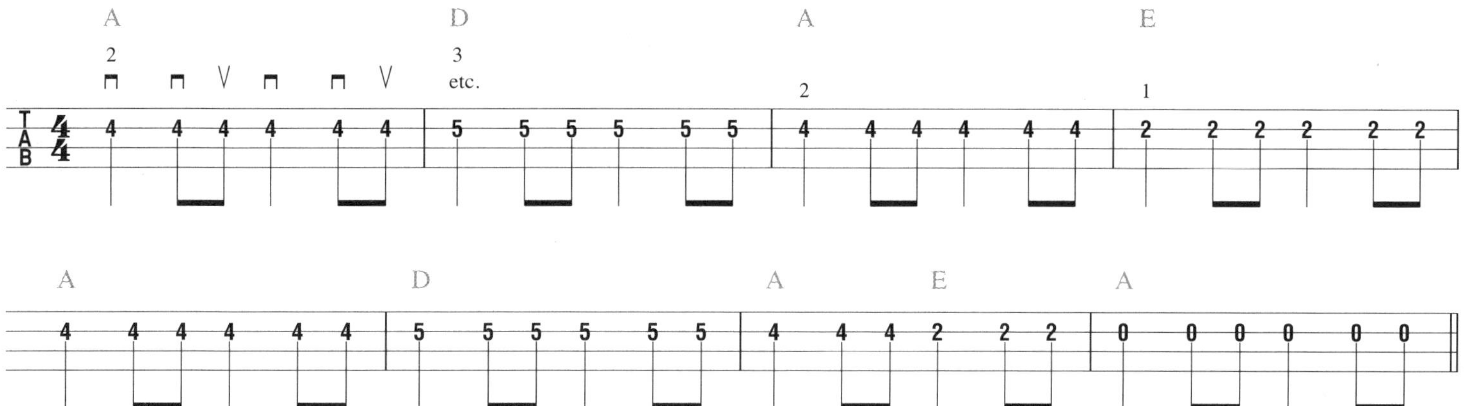

TOOLBOX

Double-stops

To make solos on the mandolin sound more interesting, we often play a harmony note along with a melody note. Traditionally, fiddle players refer to this as a *double-stop*. Including double-stops is a great way to build up a melody or solo, helping it to sound more intricate and developed.

In "Boil Them Cabbage Down," we can take the same exact melody that we've been using on the A string and add some harmony notes on the E string to create double-stops. Most of the harmony notes will just be the open E string, but the 2nd fret of the E string will also be used to harmonize with the melody notes on the 5th fret. At first, it can be very difficult to play a fretted note on the A string without unintentionally touching the E string. You'll need to practice arching over the E string with your finger to make sure you can always hear two distinct notes on each and every pick stroke. Let's give it a try!

BOIL THEM CABBAGE DOWN

Double-stops

American Folksong

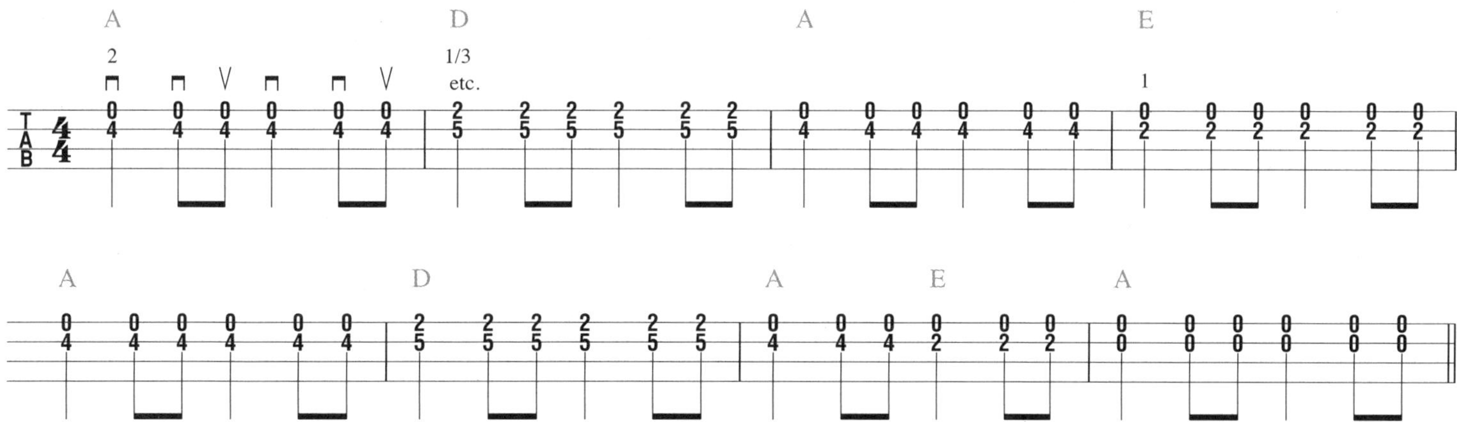

In the next variation, we'll mix in a series of eighth-note runs or licks in between measures of shuffle-pattern double-stops. Measures 1, 3, and 5 (the first three measures that originally included the 4th fret in the melody on the A string) have been replaced with the same lick. This lick was created by including notes above and below the 4th fret in the A major scale: the 5th fret, 2nd fret, and open string. The next to last measure has been replaced with its own lick using just the notes at or below the 4th fret.

BOIL THEM CABBAGE DOWN

Added Runs

American Folksong

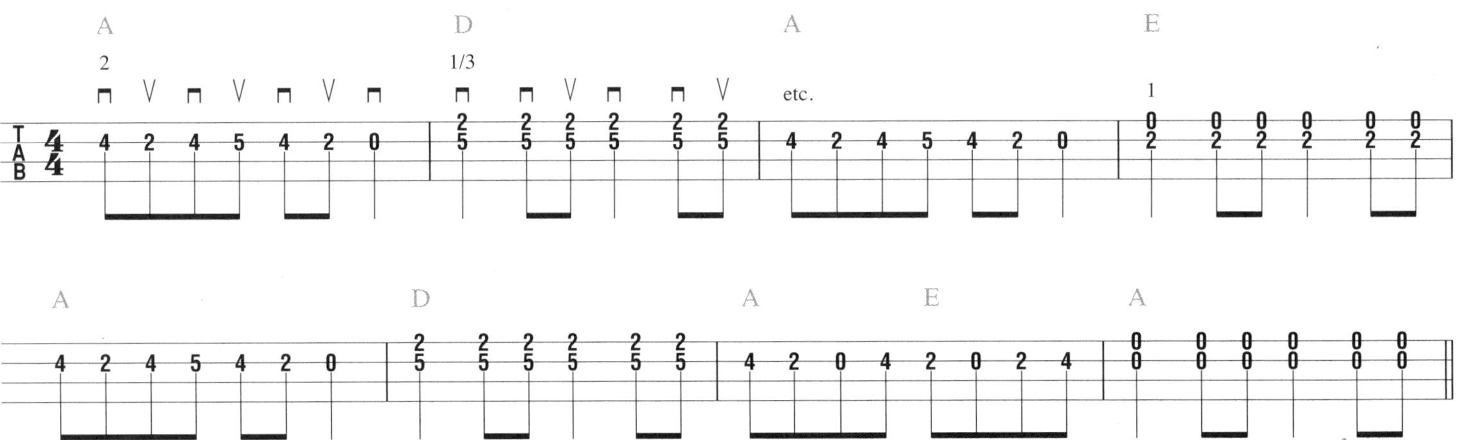

Finally, we can play runs in every measure while bouncing around the notes of the basic melody to develop a solo. Notice that you'll be playing the 6th fret on the D string with your third finger in the next to last measure. For all other fingerings, simply remember that the 1st and 2nd frets are fretted with your first (or index) finger, the 3rd and 4th frets with your second (or middle) finger, the 5th and 6th frets with your third (or ring) finger, and the 7th fret with your fourth (or pinky) finger.

BOIL THEM CABBAGE DOWN

Developed Solo

American Folksong

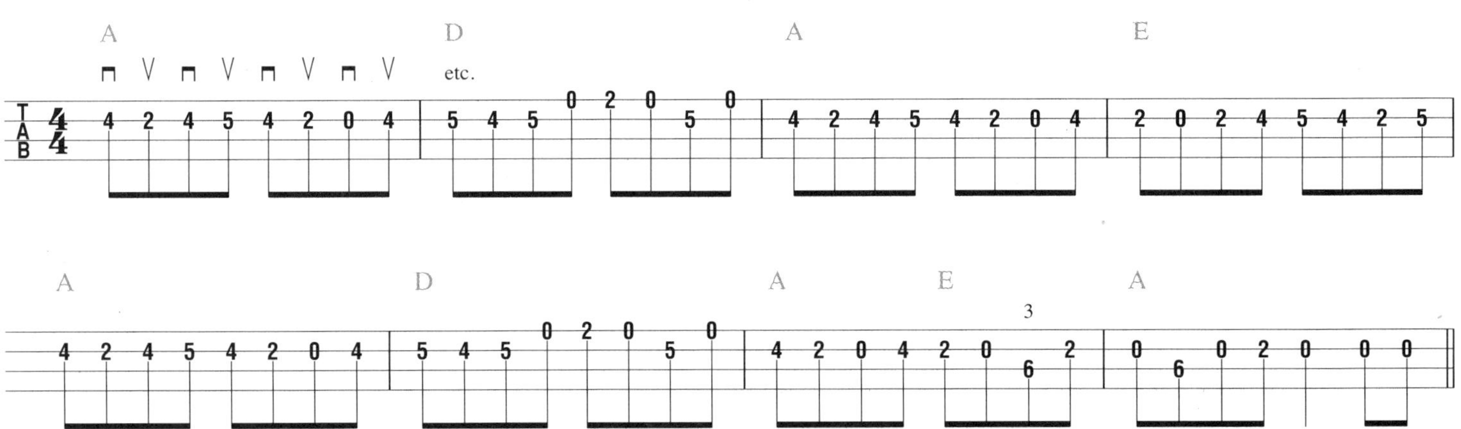

TOOLBOX

A and B Parts

A typical fiddle tune melody consists of two parts known as the A part and the B part, with each part played twice in succession. For example, you would play the A part twice before moving on and playing the B part twice (AA-BB.) To indicate this repetition without writing out the same part twice, repeat signs are used. These signs, which look like colons, are placed at the beginning and end of each part. Once you reach the repeat sign at the end of a part, look back for the nearest starting repeat sign, go back to it, and start again from there. After playing through the section a second time, move on to the next part.

Now let's go through a similar process with another fiddle tune, "Cripple Creek," building licks on the basic melody across different versions of the tune. By this point, you should understand that we're using downstrokes on the downbeats and upstrokes on the upbeats, so those symbols will be included in the music sparingly moving forward.

CRIPPLE CREEK

Basic Melody

American Fiddle Tune

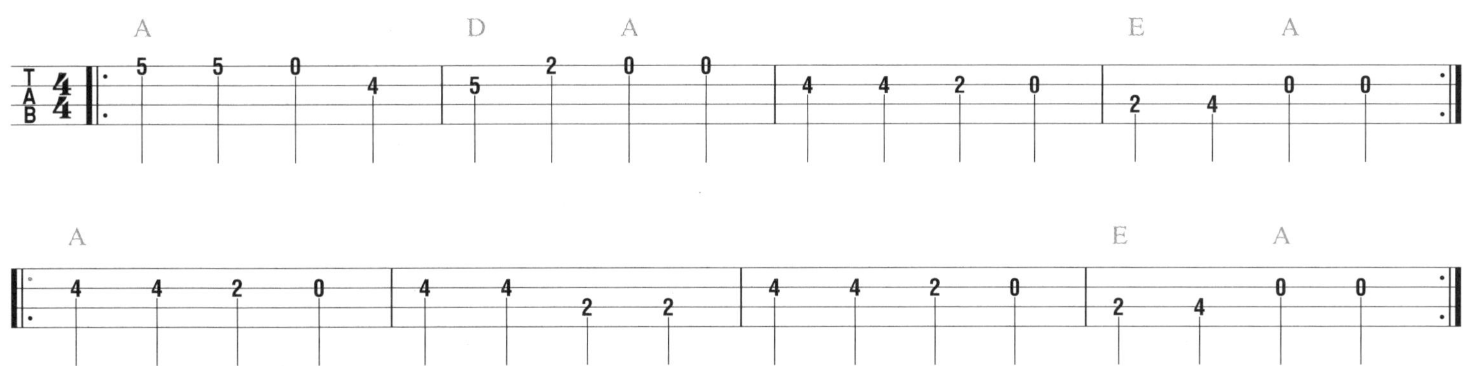

CRIPPLE CREEK

Developed Solo 1

American Fiddle Tune

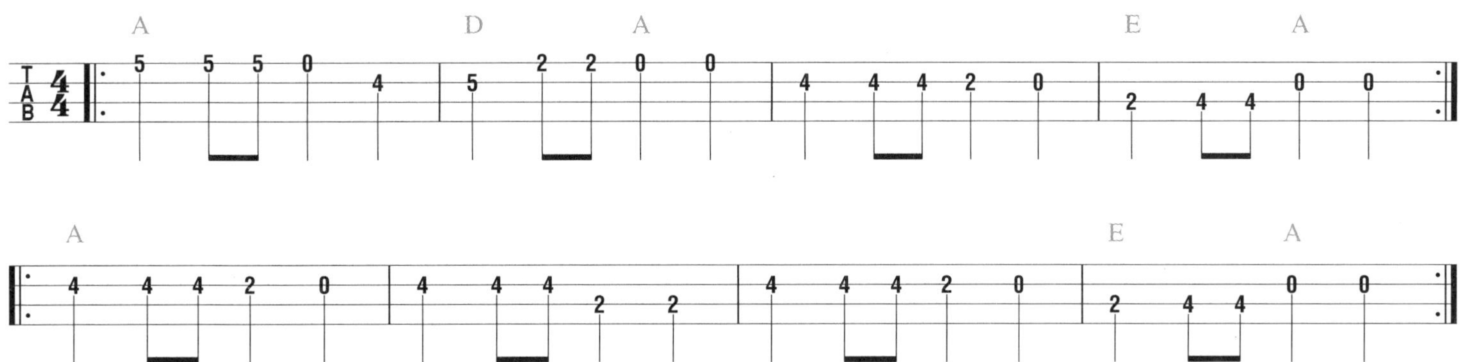

CRIPPLE CREEK

Developed Solo 2

American Fiddle Tune

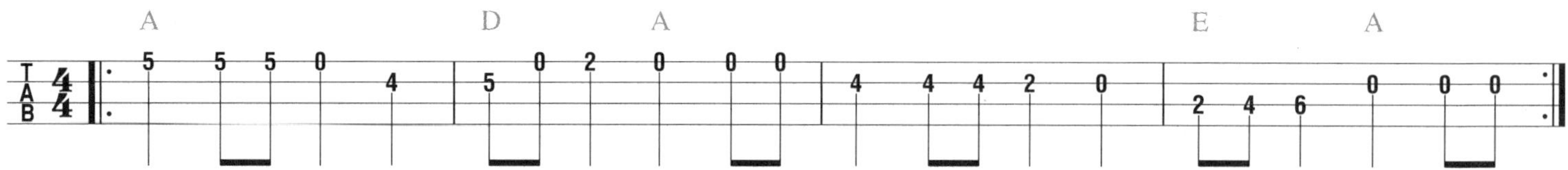

CRIPPLE CREEK

Developed Solo 3

American Fiddle Tune

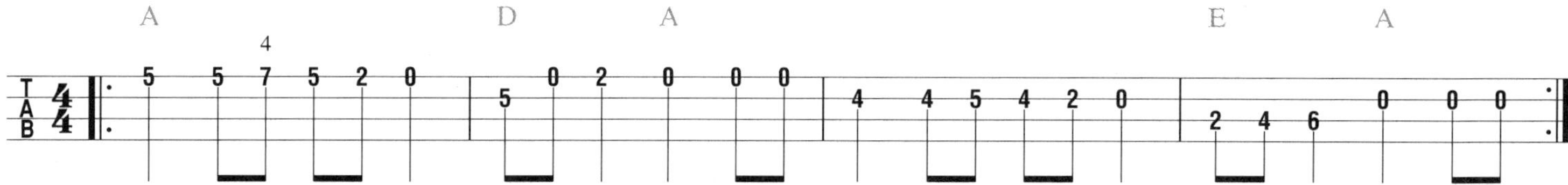

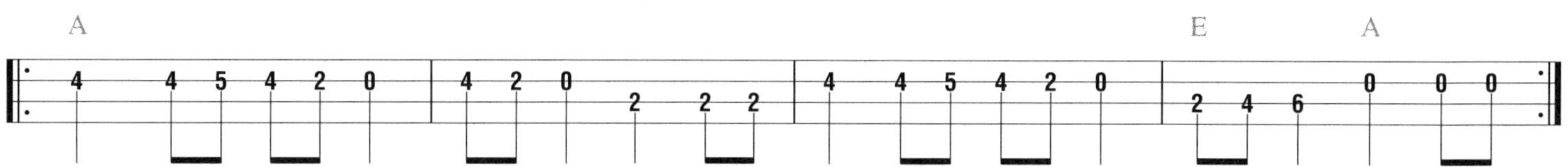

CRIPPLE CREEK

Developed Solo 4

American Fiddle Tune

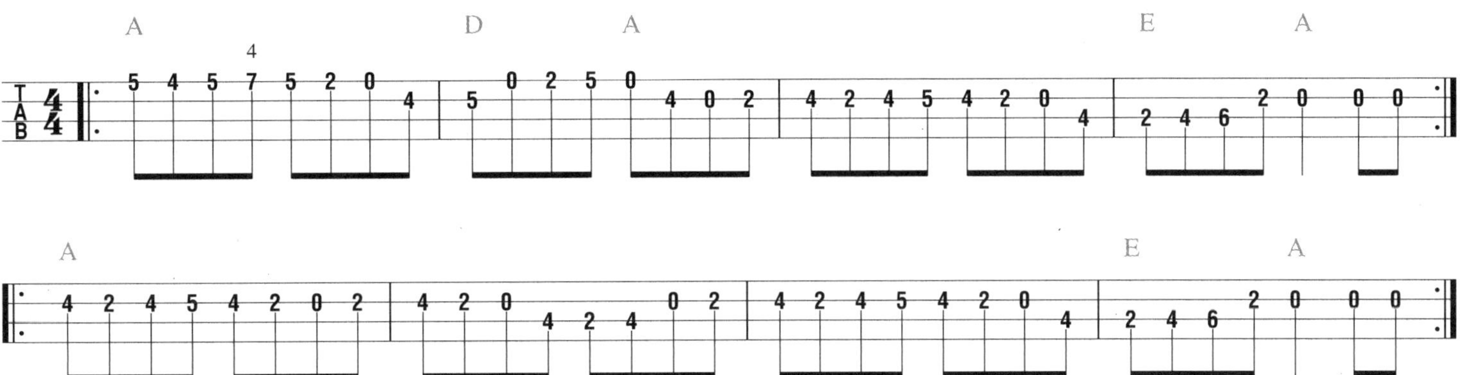

We'll try building on one more fiddle tune, "Old Joe Clark," starting with the basic melody.

OLD JOE CLARK

Basic Melody

Tennessee Folksong

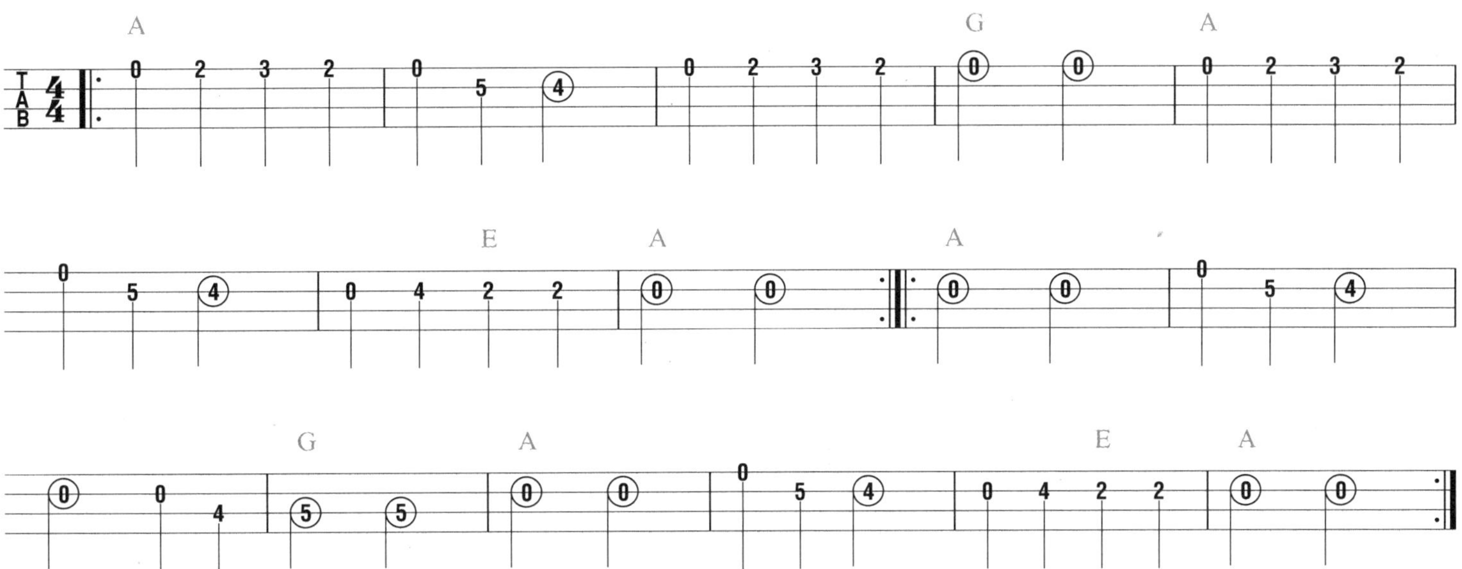

TOOLBOX

Pickup Measures & First and Second Endings

In the next arrangement, do you notice that the measure before the very first repeat sign contains only two eighth notes? This incomplete measure is called a *pickup measure*. The notes in this measure, called *pickup notes*, are played at the end of the pickup measure, not on the first beat.

You'll also see brackets containing the numbers "1" and "2" above some of the measures. These are known as *first and second endings*. We use these, along with repeat signs, to transition smoothly from one part to another whenever it's necessary to change a couple of the notes that were used at the end the first time through. So instead of rewriting an entire part and just changing a few notes at the end, we can use first and second endings, and which ending you play depends on whether it's your first or second time playing through the part.

In this next solo, we'll use our familiar shuffle pattern to build out the melody. Notice that the piece begins with two pickup notes. To determine which beat to start on in the pickup measure, take a look at the note values of the pickup notes. In this case, we can see that the two eighth notes on the 4th and 5th fret would have to fall on the "4 and" of the pickup measure. So, you would count "1, 2, 3" and then start playing on beat 4. You can also look at the rests in the pickup measure to figure out how many beats you'll need to wait before playing the first note. Here, we have a *half rest*, a new type of rest that equals two beats, followed by a quarter rest, meaning that we rest for a total of three beats before playing the first note on beat 4.

We'll also use a few first and second endings. The first time through the A part, play the first ending. Then, since we have a repeat sign at the end of the first ending, go back to the repeat sign at the beginning and play the A part again. However, this time around, skip the first ending (the music under the "1" bracket) and proceed directly to the second ending (the music under the "2" bracket). Finally, notice that we're using a second set of first and second endings in the B part to help close the piece. When you get to the repeat sign in this first ending, go back to the nearest forward-facing repeat sign (not the one at the very beginning) and then play through to the second ending, skipping the first ending. Watch the accompanying video to get a better idea of how this is all done.

OLD JOE CLARK

Solo 2

Tennessee Folksong

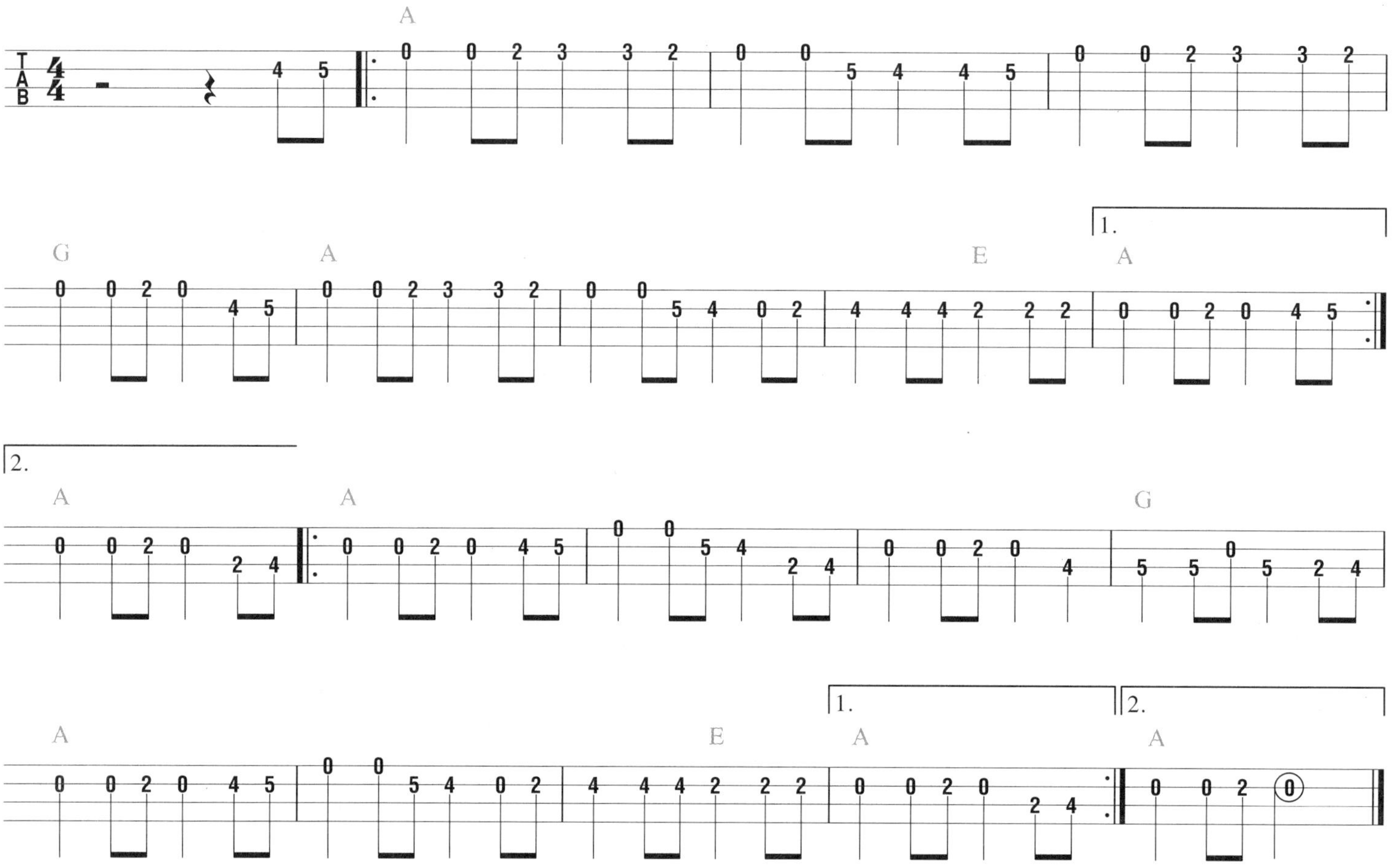

A G A E 1. A 2. A A G A E 1. A 2. A

Last but not least, let's turn the melody of "Old Joe Clark" into a developed solo.

OLD JOE CLARK

Solo 3

Tennessee Folksong

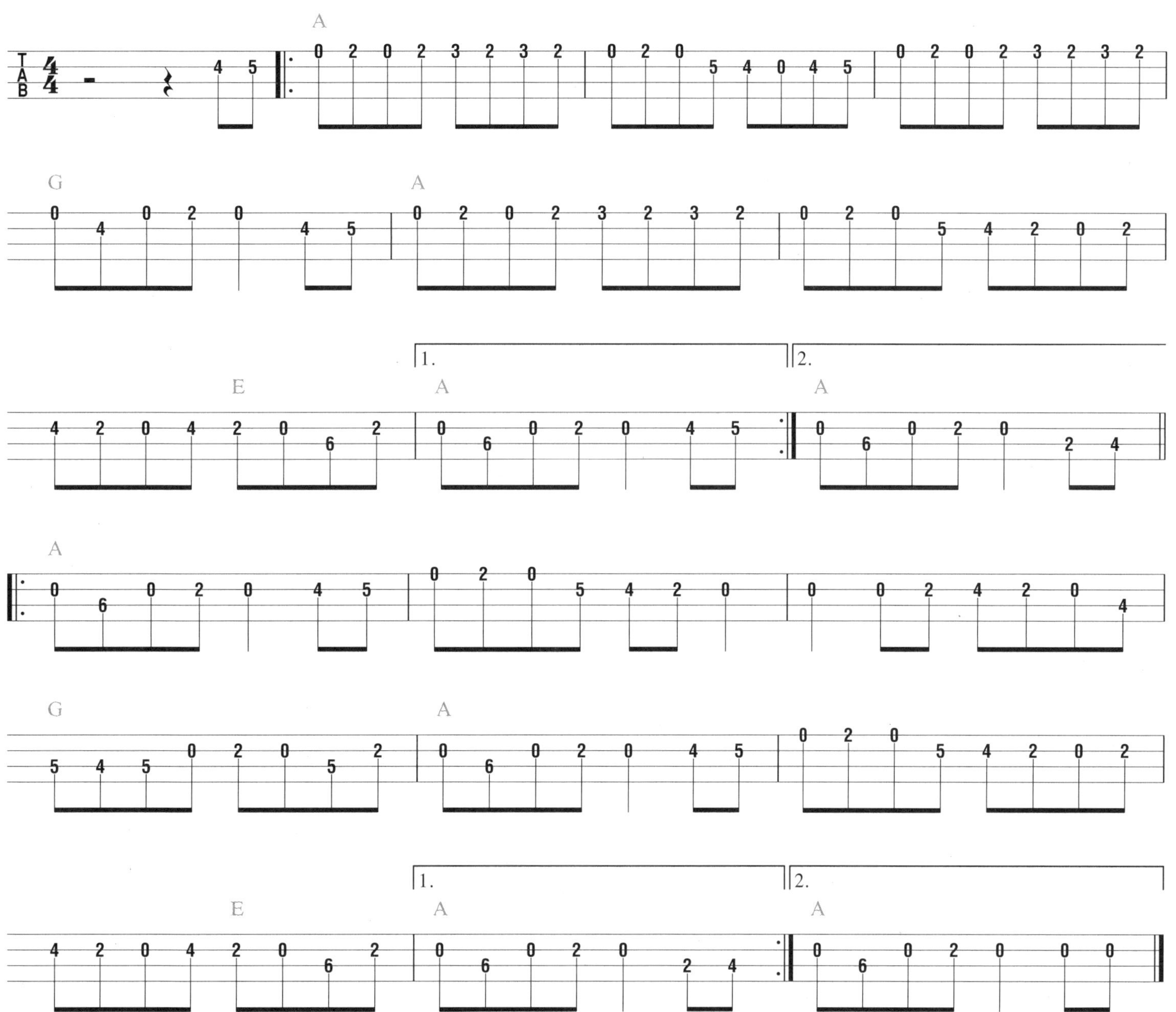

Let's try one more. To help make this next song sound more musical, try holding down the 2nd fret for the entire first measure to let it sustain along with the open A string, rather than cutting it short by lifting your finger between each note. Do the same with the notes at the 2nd and 3rd frets in the third measure (which is just a two-finger G chord). Finally, in the first and second endings of the A part—as well as in the first ending of the B part—hold the 5th fret of the A string down until the fourth beat; in the second ending of the B part, hold it down until the end.

LIBERTY

Solo 1

Traditional

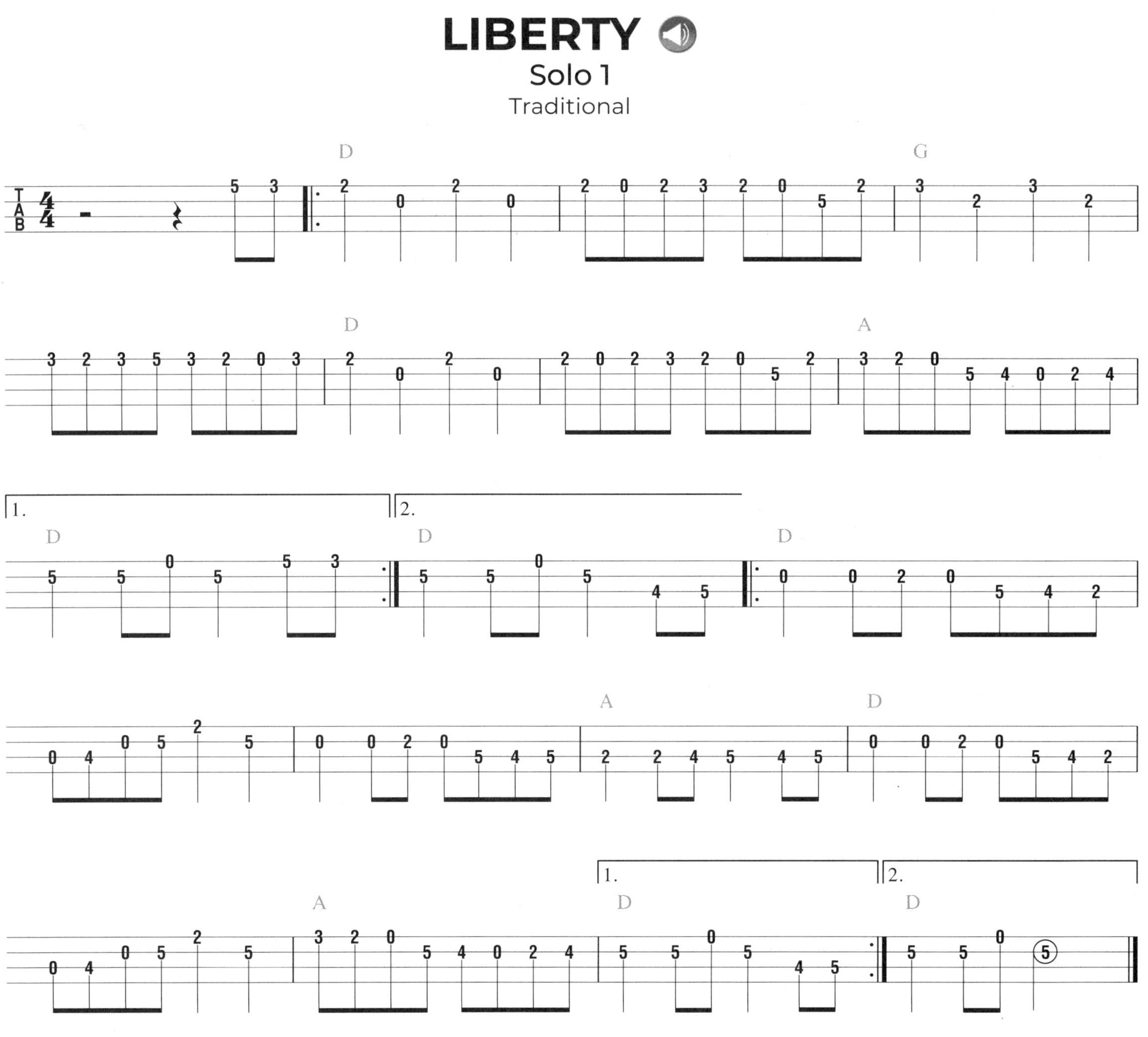

The second version of "Liberty" is a developed solo that includes more eighth-note runs. Watch the video for a demonstration.

LIBERTY

Solo 2

Traditional

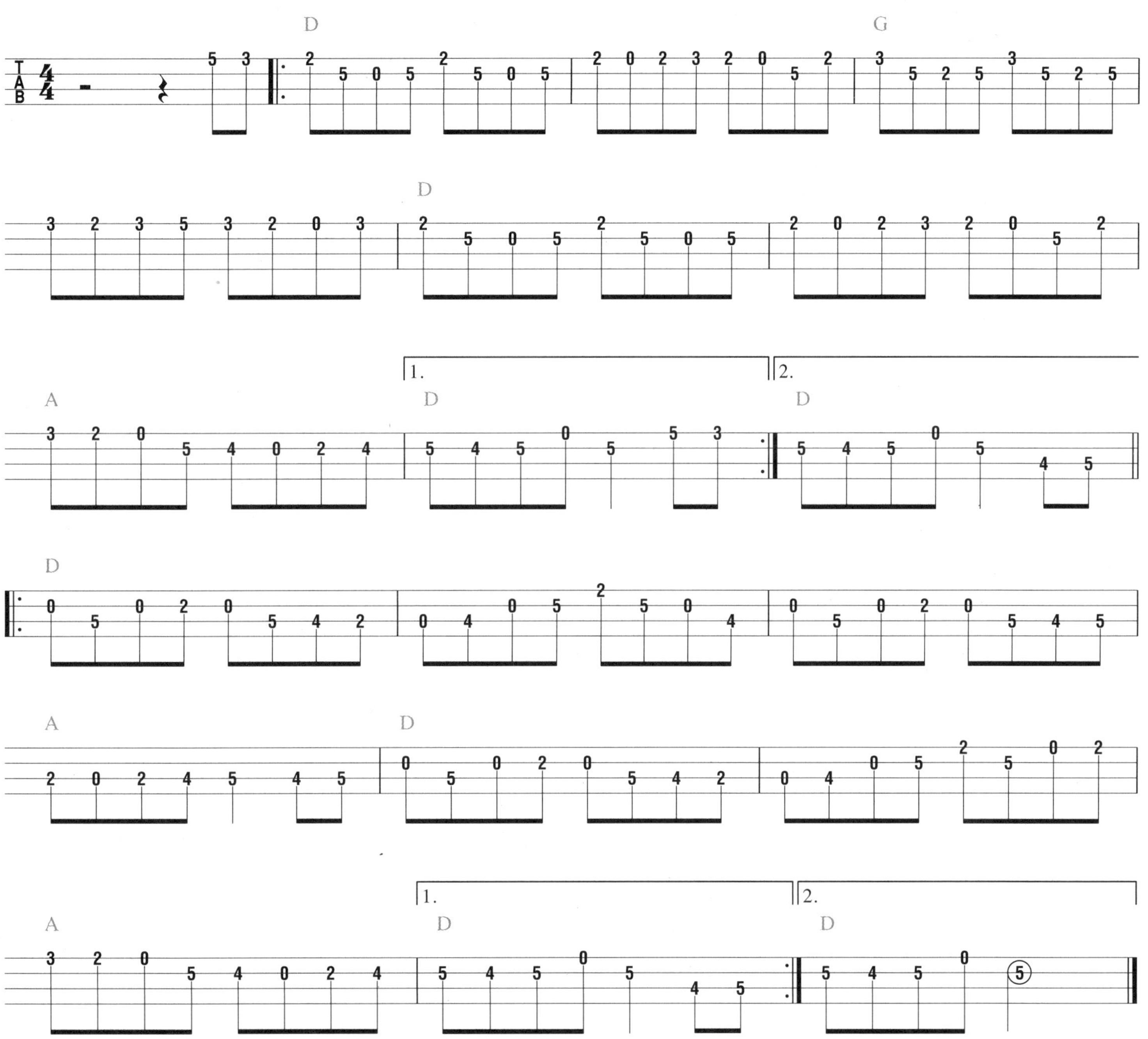

Chapter 6:
More Strumming Patterns

Strumming on beats 2 and 4, as discussed in chapter 3, isn't the only way you can strum chords. Here are a few more strumming patterns to try out. If you'd like to try playing along with the video, use the following open G, C, and D chords and play them in this order: G-C-D-G. In all three of the strumming patterns demonstrated, you'll play through the pattern twice for each chord. (**Note:** The chord shapes used on the video for these chords will be taught later on in the book.)

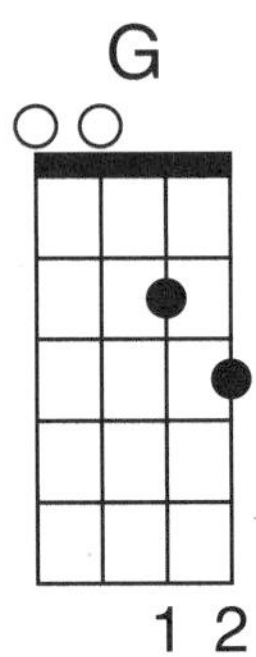

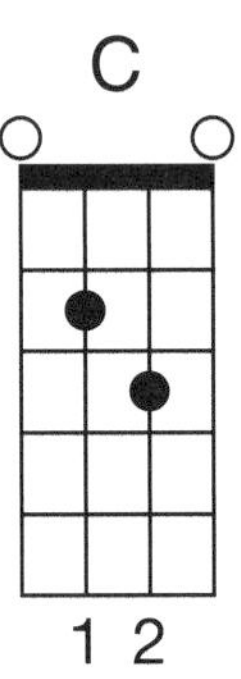

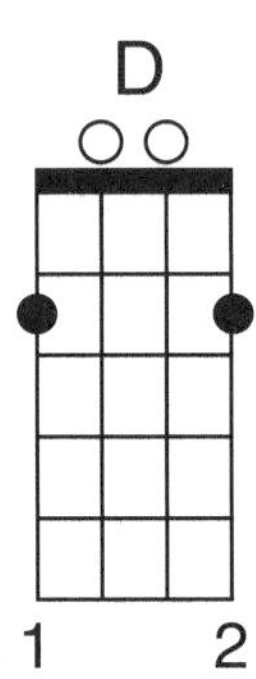

Strumming Pattern 1

Strumming Pattern 2

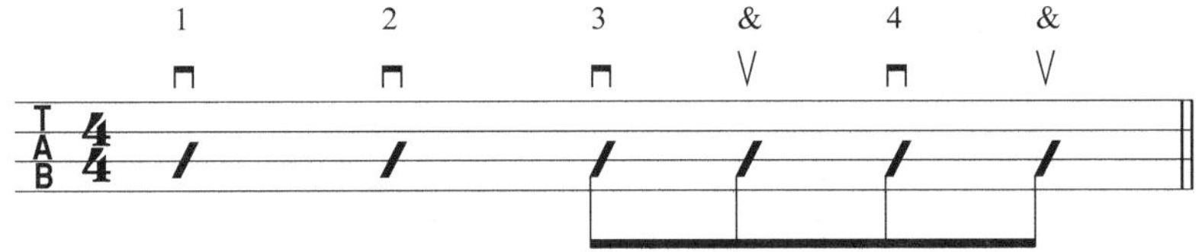

Strumming Pattern 3

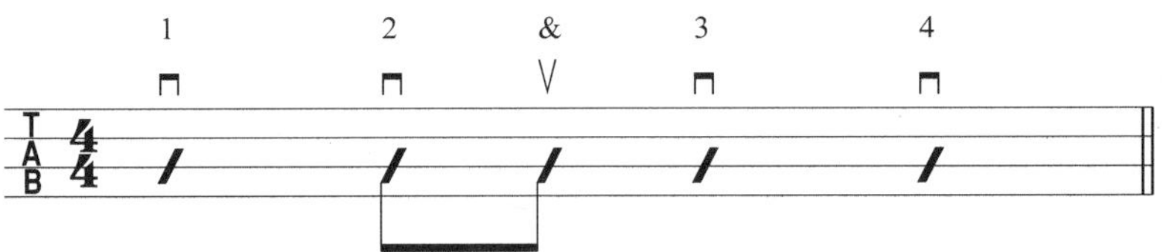

Let's try these new patterns in a few songs.

BLUE EYES CRYING IN THE RAIN

Strumming Pattern 1

Words and Music by Fred Rose

C *(4 m.)*
In the twilight glow I see her,

G *(2 m.)* **C** *(2 m.)*
Blue eyes cryin' in the rain.

C *(4 m.)*
When we kissed goodbye and parted,

G *(2 m.)* **C** *(2 m.)*
I knew we'd never meet again.

F *(4 m.)*
Love is like a dying ember,

C *(2 m.)* **G** *(2 m.)*
And only memories remain.

C *(4 m.)*
And through the ages I'll remember

G *(2 m.)* **C** *(4 m.)*
Blue eyes crying in the rain.

F *(4 m.)*
Some day when we meet up yonder,

C *(2 m.)* **G** *(2 m.)*
We'll stroll hand in hand again

C *(4 m.)*
In a land that knows no parting,

G *(2 m.)* **C** *(2 m.)*
Blue eyes crying in the rain.

I WALK THE LINE

Strumming pattern 3

Words and Music by Johnny Cash

G *(2 m.)* **C** *(2 m.)*
I keep a close watch on this heart of mine.

G *(2 m.)* **C** *(2 m.)*
I keep my eyes wide open all the time.

F *(2 m.)* **C** *(2 m.)*
I keep the ends out for the tie that binds.

G *(2 m.)* **C** *(2 m.)*
Because you're mine, I walk the line.

WILL THE CIRCLE BE UNBROKEN

Strumming pattern 2

Words by Ada R. Habershon
Music by Charles H. Gabriel

```
     C (4 m.)
I was standing by my window
        F (2 m.)        C (2 m.)
On one cold and cloudy day,
        C (4 m.)
When I saw that hearse come rolling
      C (1 m.)   G (1 m.)  C (2 m.)
For to carry my mother away.

        C (4 m.)
Will the circle be unbroken
        F (2 m.)        C (2 m.)
By and by, Lord, by and by?
          C (4 m.)
There's a better home a-waiting
      C (1 m.)   G (1 m.) C (1 m.)
In the sky, Lord, in the  sky.
```


More Chords

For the C, G, and F chords we've played, have you noticed that the shape you make with your fingers on the fretboard stays the same even though the chords are played on different strings? Well, you can also move the same shape up the neck, on the same strings, to play any other chord on the mandolin, as long as you take care to just play the two notes you're holding down. For example, if you move the C chord up two frets, you're playing a D chord; two frets higher is an E chord; one more fret and you have an F chord. (**Note:** When you see a number plus "fr" near the top of a chord chart, instead of a thick line, it means that the chord is formed starting at the fret indicated, not down by the nut; for example, the D chord shown here uses the 4th fret of the D string and the 5th fret of the A string.)

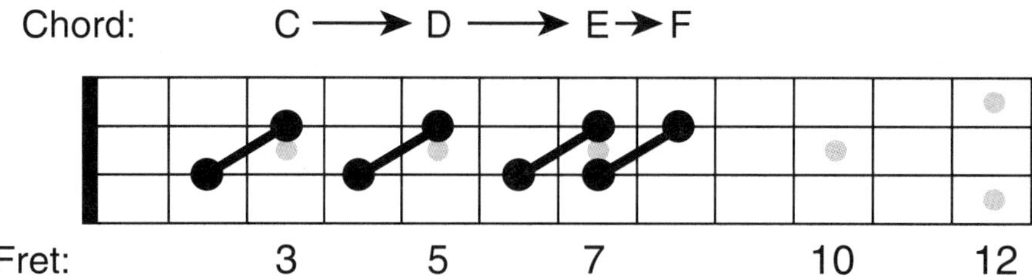

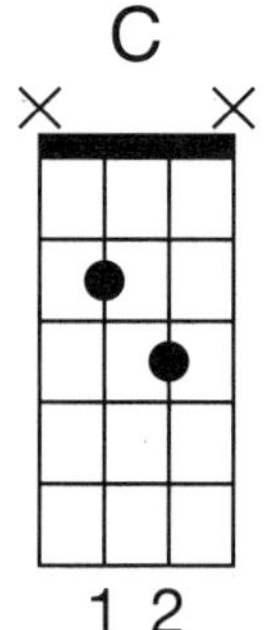

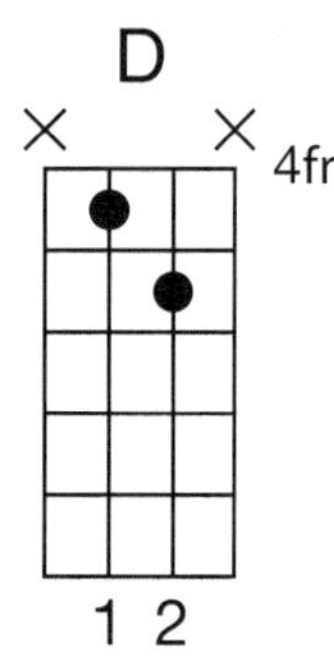

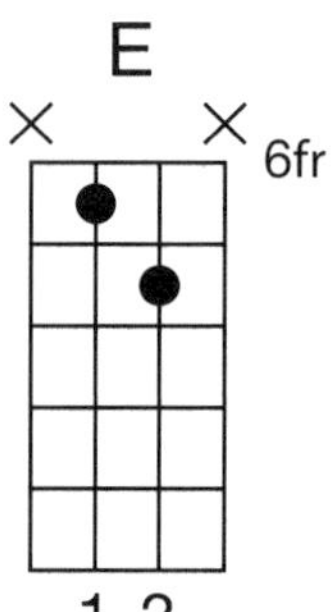

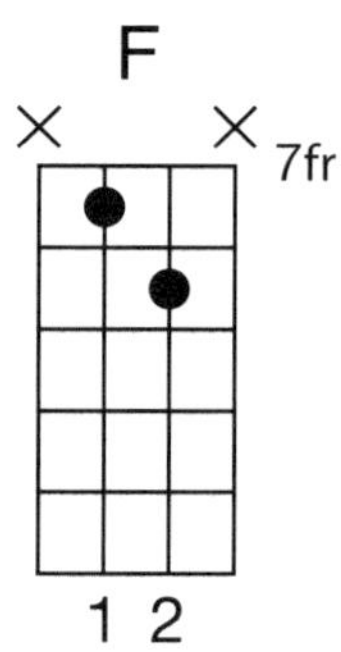

Starting with the G chord, we can move two frets higher to play an A chord, two more frets for B, and one more fret for C. (**Note**: This C chord with its root on the E string includes the same two notes as the C chord we've been playing on the A string, just played on different strings). With this type of chord, the shape we make with our first and second finger never changes.

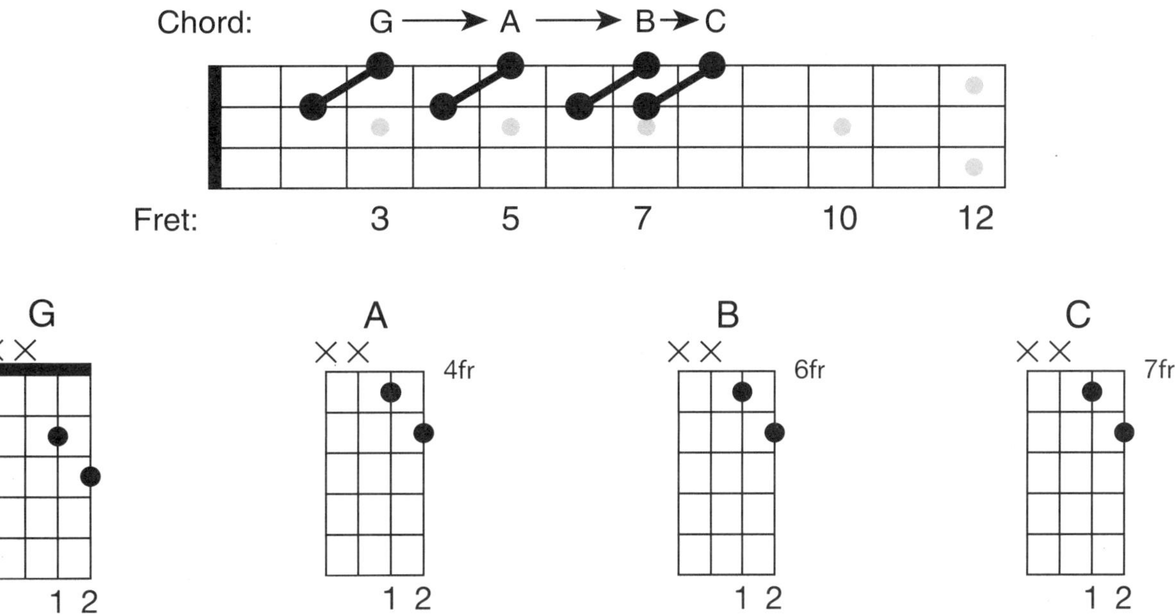

So far, we've been exclusively using *major chords*. But *minor chords* are just as easy to play, and it's simple to turn the major bluegrass chord shape into the minor shape. To turn any of these two-note major chords into a minor chord, all you have to do is pull your first finger back one fret. It's that easy! Give it a try yourself by first making a G chord. Then, pull your first finger back to the 1st fret without moving your middle finger—this a G minor chord (Gm).

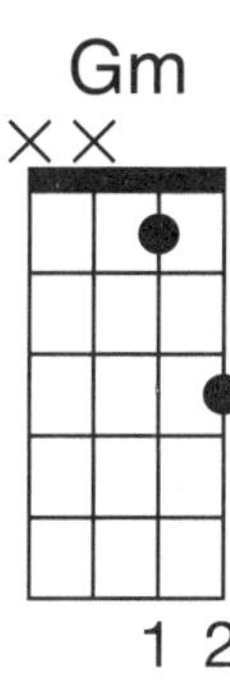

The same can be done with any major chop chord. Here are the other minor chords that you'll be using in the upcoming songs.

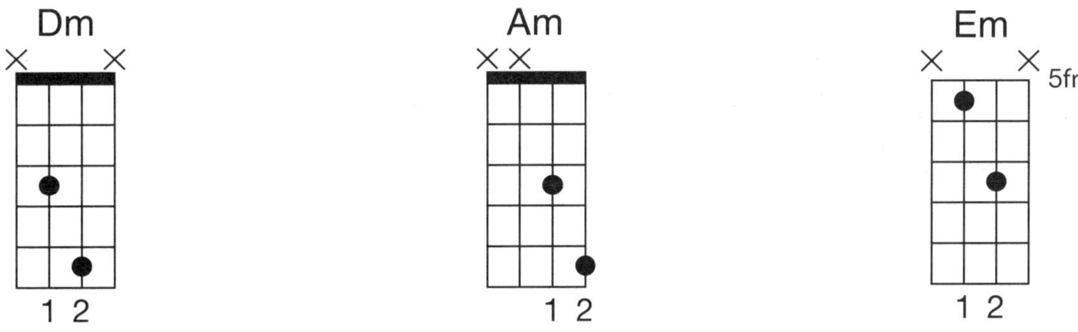

Learning where to place these shapes on the fretboard to play every two-finger chord as either major or minor will allow you to play almost any song that you're familiar with. Watch the accompanying video for more on these moveable chord shapes.

Let's try a few tunes using some of our new chords. In "Your Cheatin' Heart," you'll hear a variation of Strumming Pattern 1 on the audio. To match this rhythm, you won't play on the downbeat of beat 3. Instead, skip the downstroke on beat 3 and start playing again with an upstroke on beat "3 and." The rest of the pattern is the same.

YOUR CHEATIN' HEART

Words and Music by Hank Williams

C *(2 m.)* **F** *(2 m.)*
Your cheatin' heart will make you weep.

G *(2 m.)* **C** *(2 m.)*
You'll cry and cry and try to sleep.

C *(2 m.)* **F** *(2 m.)*
But sleep won't come the whole night through.

G *(2 m.)* **C** *(2 m.)*
Your cheatin' heart will tell on you.

F *(2 m.)* **C** *(2 m.)*
When tears come down like fallin' rain,

D *(2 m.)* **G** *(2 m.)*
You'll toss around and call my name.

C *(2 m.)* **F** *(2 m.)*
You'll walk the floor the way I do.

G *(2 m.)* **C** *(2 m.)*
Your cheatin' heart will tell on you.

For the remaining songs in this chapter, you'll hear a "chop rhythm" used on the audio, as taught in chapter 3. This is a good place to start, but feel free to try the other strumming patterns you learned in this chapter for practice.

POOR WAYFARING STRANGER

Traditional Folksong

Am *(4 m.)*
I'm just a poor wayfaring stranger,

Dm *(2 m.)* **Am** *(2 m.)*
Traveling through this world below.

Am *(4 m.)*
There's no sickness, no toil or danger,

Dm *(1 m.)* **E** *(1 m.)* **Am** *(2 m.)*
In that bright land to which I go.

F *(2 m.)* **C** *(2 m.)*
I'm going there to see my father

F *(2 m.)* **E** *(2 m.)*
And all my loved ones, who've gone on.

Am *(4 m.)*
I'm just going over Jordan.

Dm *(1 m.)* **E** *(1 m.)* **Am** *(2 m.)*
I'm just going over home.

ROCKY TOP

Words and Music by Boudleaux Bryant and Felice Bryant

G *(2 m.)* **C** *(1 m.)* **G** *(1 m.)*
Wish that I was on ol' Rocky Top,

Em *(1 m.)* **D** *(1 m.)* **G** *(2 m.)*
Down in the Tennessee hills.

G *(2 m.)* **C** *(1 m.)* **G** *(1 m.)*
Ain't no smoggy smoke on Rocky Top,

Em *(1 m.)* **D** *(1 m.)* **G** *(2 m.)*
Ain't no telephone bills.

G *(2 m.)* **C** *(1 m.)* **G** *(1 m.)*
Once I had a girl on Rocky Top,

Em *(1 m.)* **D** *(1 m.)* **G** *(2 m.)*
Half bear, other half cat.

G *(2 m.)* **C** *(1 m.)* **G** *(1 m.)*
Wild as a mink but sweet as soda pop,

Em *(1 m.)* **D** *(1 m.)* **G** *(2 m.)*
I still dream about that.

Em *(2 m.)* **D** *(2 m.)*
Rocky Top, you'll always be

F *(2 m.)* **C** *(2 m.)*
Home sweet home to me.

C *(2 m.)* **G** *(2 m.)*
Good ol' Rocky Top,

G *(1 m.)* **F** *(1 m.)* **G** *(2 m.)*
Rocky Top, Tennessee,

G *(1 m.)* **F** *(1 m.)* **G** *(2 m.)*
Rocky Top, Tennessee.

An F♯m chord will be used in the next two songs. Notice that we again see a fret indicator, not a thick line representing the nut of the mandolin, near the top line of the chord chart—this time it's "7fr." So, for the F♯m chop chord, you'll fret the 9th fret of the A string with your second finger, and the 7th fret of the D string with your first finger. Always watch out for these fret indicators when learning new chords!

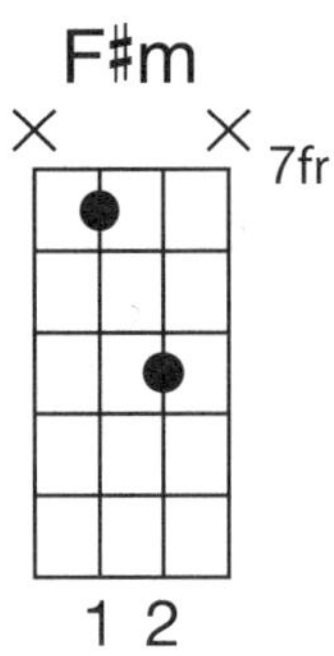

TAKE ME HOME, COUNTRY ROADS

Words and Music by John Denver, Bill Danoff and Taffy Nivert

A *(2 m.)* **F♯m** *(2 m.)*
Almost heaven, West Virginia,

E *(2 m.)* **D** *(1 m.)* **A** *(2 m.)*
Blue Ridge Mountains, Shenandoah River.

A *(2 m.)* **F♯m** *(2 m.)*
Life is old there, older than the trees,

E *(2 m.)* **D** *(1 m.)* **A** *(1 m.)*
Younger than the mountains, growin' like the breeze.

A *(2 m.)* **E** *(2 m.)*
Country roads, take me home

F♯m *(2 m.)* **D** *(2 m.)*
To the place I belong:

A *(2 m.)* **E** *(2 m.)*
West Virginia, mountain momma,

D *(2 m.)* **A** *(2 m.)*
Take me home, country roads.

A *(2 m.)* **F♯m** *(2 m.)*
All my mem'ries gather 'round her,

E *(2 m.)* **D** *(1 m.)* **A** *(2 m.)*
Miner's lady, stranger to blue water.

A *(2 m.)* **F♯m** *(2 m.)*
Dark and dusty, painted on the sky,

E *(2 m.)* **D** *(1 m.)* **A** *(1 m.)*
Misty taste of moonshine, teardrop in my eye.

A *(2 m.)* **E** *(2 m.)*
Country roads, take me home

F♯m *(2 m.)* **D** *(2 m.)*
To the place I belong:

A *(2 m.)* **E** *(2 m.)*
West Virginia, mountain momma,

D *(2 m.)* **A** *(2 m.)*
Take me home, country roads.

F♯m *(1 m.)* **E** *(1 m.)* **A** *(2 m.)*
I hear her voice, in the mornin' hour she calls me,

D *(1 m.)* **A** *(1 m.)* **E** *(2 m.)*
The radio reminds me of my home far away,

F♯m *(1 m.)* **G** *(1 m.)* **D** *(1 m.)*
And drivin' down the road I get a feelin'

A *(1 m.)* **E** *(4 m.)*
That I should've been home yesterday, yesterday.

A *(2 m.)* **E** *(2 m.)*
Country roads, take me home

F♯m *(2 m.)* **D** *(2 m.)*
To the place I belong:

A *(2 m.)* **E** *(2 m.)*
West Virginia, mountain momma,

D *(2 m.)* **A** *(2 m.)* **E** *(2 m.)* **A** *(2 m.)*
Take me home, country roads.

WAGON WHEEL

Words and Music by Bob Dylan and Ketch Secor

A *(1 m.)* **E** *(1 m.)*
Headin' down south to the land of the pines,

F♯m *(1 m.)* **D** *(1 m.)*
I'm thumbin' my way out of North Caroline.

A *(1 m.)* **E** *(1 m.)* **D** *(2 m.)*
Starin' up the road and pray to God I see headlights.

A *(1 m.)* **E** *(1 m.)*
I made it down the coast in seventeen hours.

F♯m *(1 m.)* **D** *(1 m.)*
Pickin' me a bouquet of dogwood flowers.

A *(1 m.)* **E** *(1 m.)* **D** *(2 m.)*
And I'm a-hopin' for Raleigh; I can see my baby tonight.

A *(1 m.)* **E** *(1 m.)*
So, rock me, mama, like a wagon wheel.

F♯m *(1 m.)* **D** *(1 m.)*
Rock me, mama, any way you feel.

A *(1 m.)* **E** *(1 m.)* **D** *(2 m.)*
Hey, mama, rock me.

A *(1 m.)* **E** *(1 m.)*
Rock me, mama, like the wind and the rain.

F♯m *(1 m.)* **D** *(1 m.)*
Rock me, mama, like a southbound train.

A *(1 m.)* **E** *(1 m.)* **D** *(2 m.)* **A**
Hey, mama, rock me.

Chapter 7:
Slides, Hammer-ons, and Pull-offs

There are a few things that we can do on the mandolin with our fret-hand fingers to get two notes out of a single pick stroke. It's important to know how to use these common techniques, so let's not waste any time and get right into it.

Slides

A *slide* is a technique where you pluck the string while fretting a note, then while that note is still ringing, you slide that same finger up or down to a different fret. For instance, in the first measure of the following example, we start with our third finger on the 5th fret of the A string, pluck the string, and then slide up to the 7th fret without plucking the string again—one pick stroke gives us two notes. In the second measure, we again start on the 5th fret, but this time we use our second finger and slide down to the 3rd fret. For the most part, you'll start a slide with the finger that you'd normally use on the fret you're landing on. The double-stop slide in the third measure is very common on mandolin. You pluck both the A and E strings, then slide from the 5th fret to the 7th fret of the A string while the E string is still ringing. It's a clever way of "sliding into" the open E-string note that we're wanting to hear as the main note.

The slides in the first three measures of the following example are all quarter-note slides, but you can also play eighth-note slides, as shown in the final measure. For the eighth-note slides in the first half of that measure, start by using a downstroke at the 5th fret on beat 1, then slide up to the 7th fret on beat "1-and" while pretending to play an upstroke, and finally use a downstroke and then an upstroke for the two eighth notes on the open E string; do the same in the second half of the measure, but this time start the pattern with a double-stop. To help illustrate what's going on when you slide, the fret-hand fingering is shown over both notes in each slide in the following exercise. Check out the accompanying video for a demonstration of how you should approach the following slide exercises.

Slides

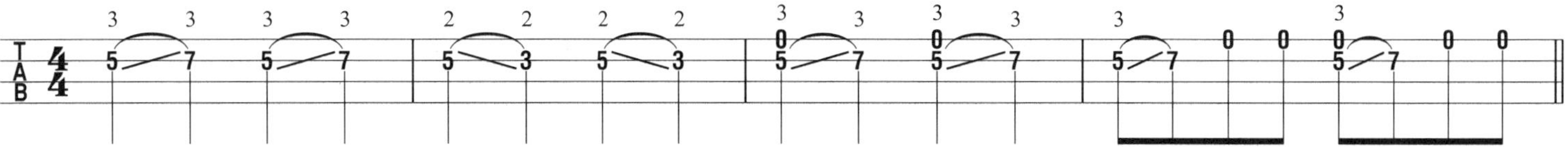

You should practice sliding with each of your first three fingers on your fret hand, as shown in the following exercise.

Sliding with Each Finger

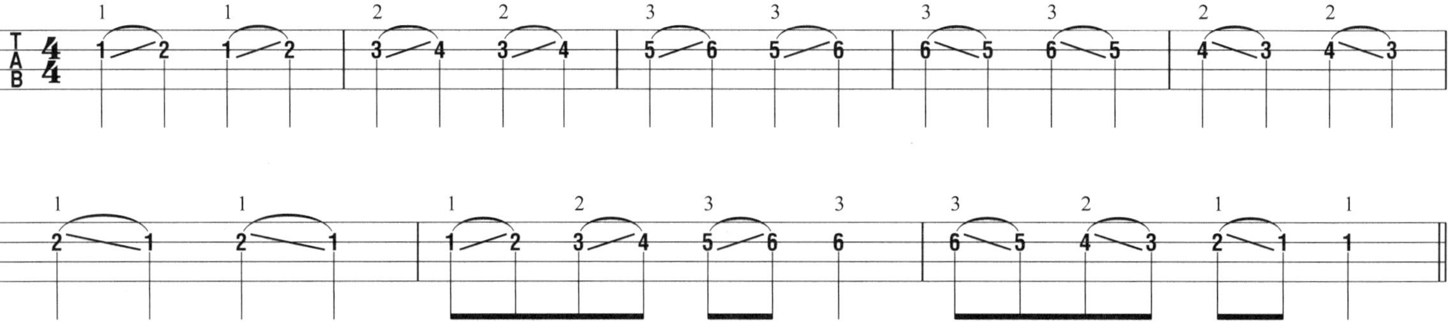

Hammer-Ons and Pull-Offs

There are a few other techniques that we can use to get two notes out of one pick stroke, but unlike slides, you'll need to use two fret-hand fingers on the same string to play them.

A *hammer-on* involves fretting a note with one finger and then "hammering-on" to a higher note on the same string with a different finger, as shown in the first measure of the next exercise. To play this hammer-on, start with your first finger on the 2nd fret of the E string, pluck it with a downstroke of your pick, and then, while the string is still ringing, "hammer" your second finger down onto the 4th fret. It takes practice to get two distinct notes, and the second note must be hit cleanly. As mentioned, it's easier to get clear notes if your fingers always land right up against the frets.

Conversely, you'll use a *pull-off* to go from a higher note to a lower one. The pull-offs in the second measure of the next exercise are accomplished by first holding down the 4th fret on the E string with your second finger—while at the same time holding your first finger down on the 2nd fret of the same string—and then plucking the string; both fingers should be down when the string is plucked. Then, you're going to pull down on the string with your second finger, the one that's been at the 4th fret, basically plucking the string as you remove your finger to ring the note below at the 2nd fret. Some players perform a pull-off by instead pushing their finger up towards the ceiling when removing it, and sometimes a player will do it one way or another depending on the line being played. In the accompanying video, I'll show you how to play through the following hammer-on and pull-off exercises.

Hammer-ons and Pull-offs Exercise 1

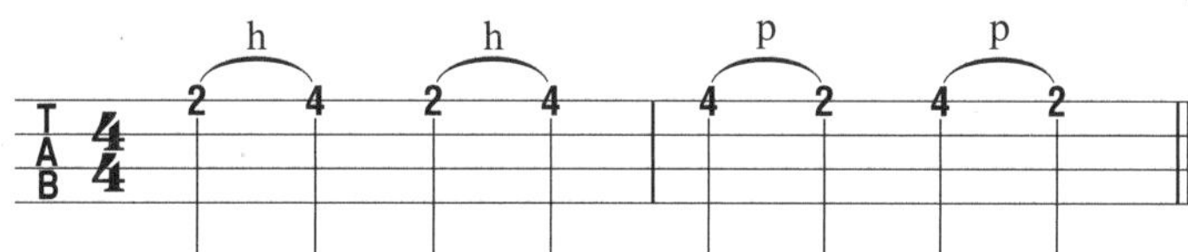

Hammer-ons and Pull-offs Exercise 2

Now, let's try a line of consecutive eighth-note hammer-ons and pull-offs.

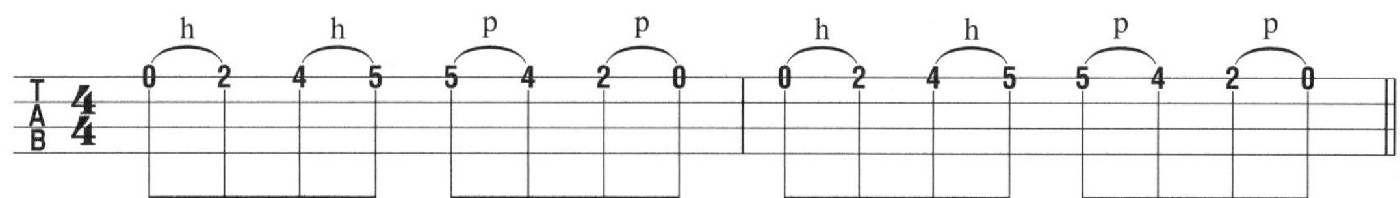

Hammer-ons and Pull-offs Exercise 3

A great way to practice hammer-ons and pull-offs with each finger is by ascending and descending through the G major scale.

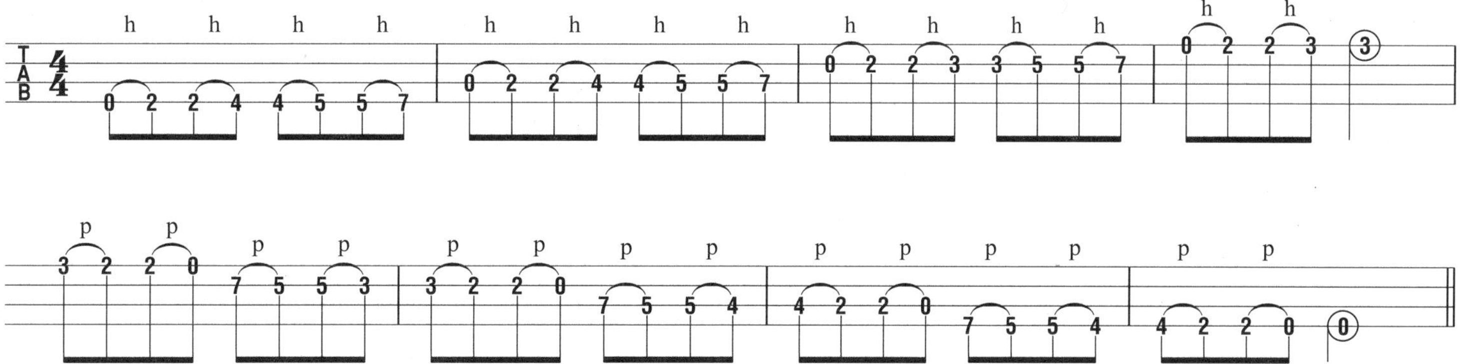

Let's try using these new techniques in a few new songs. The first one we'll look at is "Wildwood Flower." We'll start with the basic melody, as usual. Then we'll build upon the melody with slides, hammer-ons, and pull-offs. In both versions of this song, since we begin on beat 2 of the pickup measure, you'll hear me count in a full measure (1, 2, 3, 4) before giving you beat 1 of the pickup measure. This is so that the *tempo*, or the speed at which you'll play the song, is clear from the very start.

WILDWOOD FLOWER

Solo 1

Traditional

The next version of "Wildwood Flower" uses slides, hammer-ons, and pull-offs to expand on the original melody. Watch the accompanying video for a demonstration of how it's done.

WILDWOOD FLOWER

Solo 2

Traditional

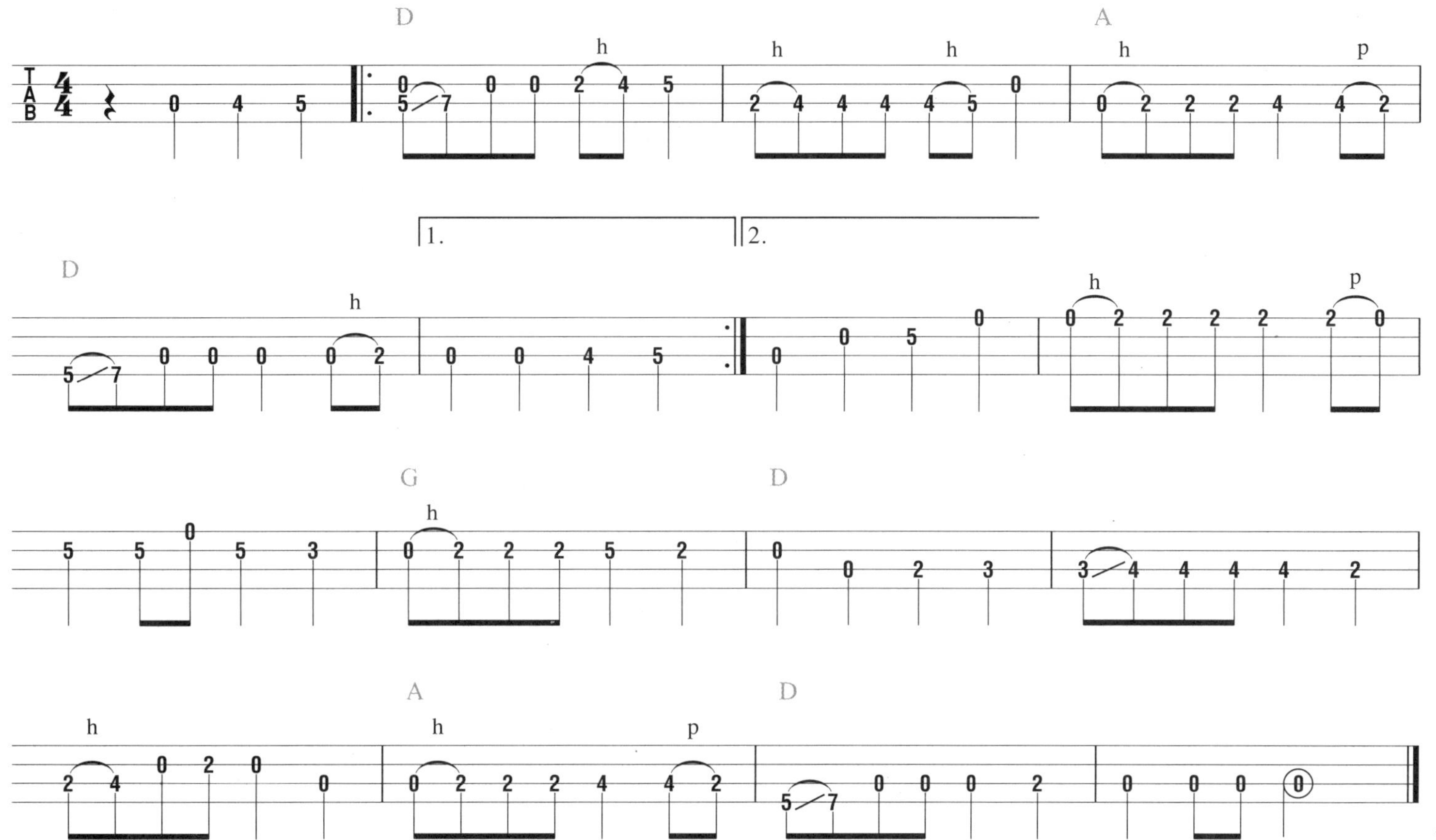

TOOLBOX

Swing Rhythm

Sometimes when playing eighth notes in a song, we need to *swing* them. What this means is that instead of keeping a straight rhythm (ta-ta-ta-ta...), you should imagine a bouncing rhythm with the first eighth note held longer than the second (taa-ta-taa-ta... or long-short-long-short...). A special indicator is normally included at the top of a piece of music letting you know that the eighth notes should be swung. Always watch for this.

The next song, "Wagon Wheel," is swung. Listen to the audio track to get a feel for how eighth notes are swung.

WAGON WHEEL

Solo 1

Words and Music by Bob Dylan and Ketch Secor

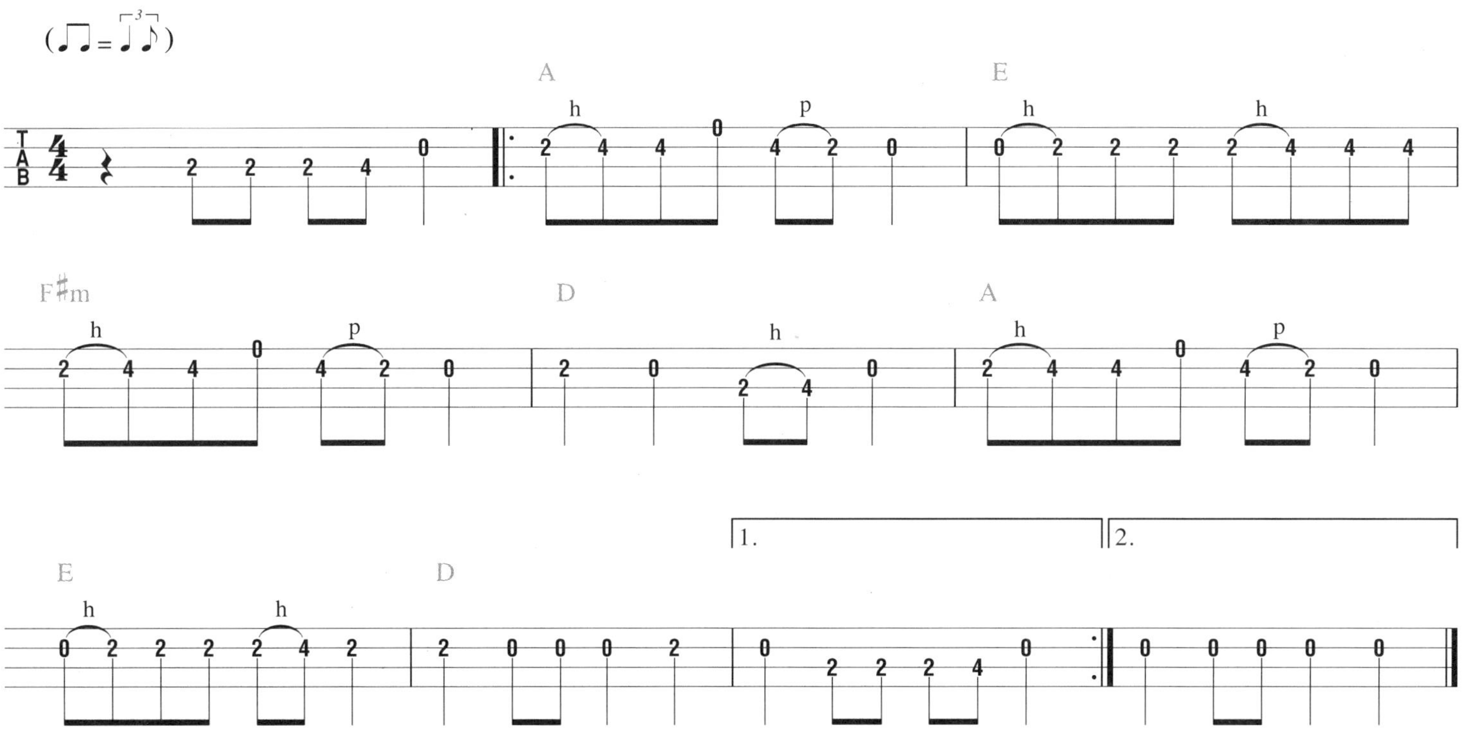

Try the same solo again, but this time, using a broader stroke with your pick, hit the open A and E strings above the melody notes as shown to create drone notes, making it sound more old-timey. Watch the accompanying video for a demonstration.

WAGON WHEEL

Solo 2

Words and Music by Bob Dylan and Ketch Secor

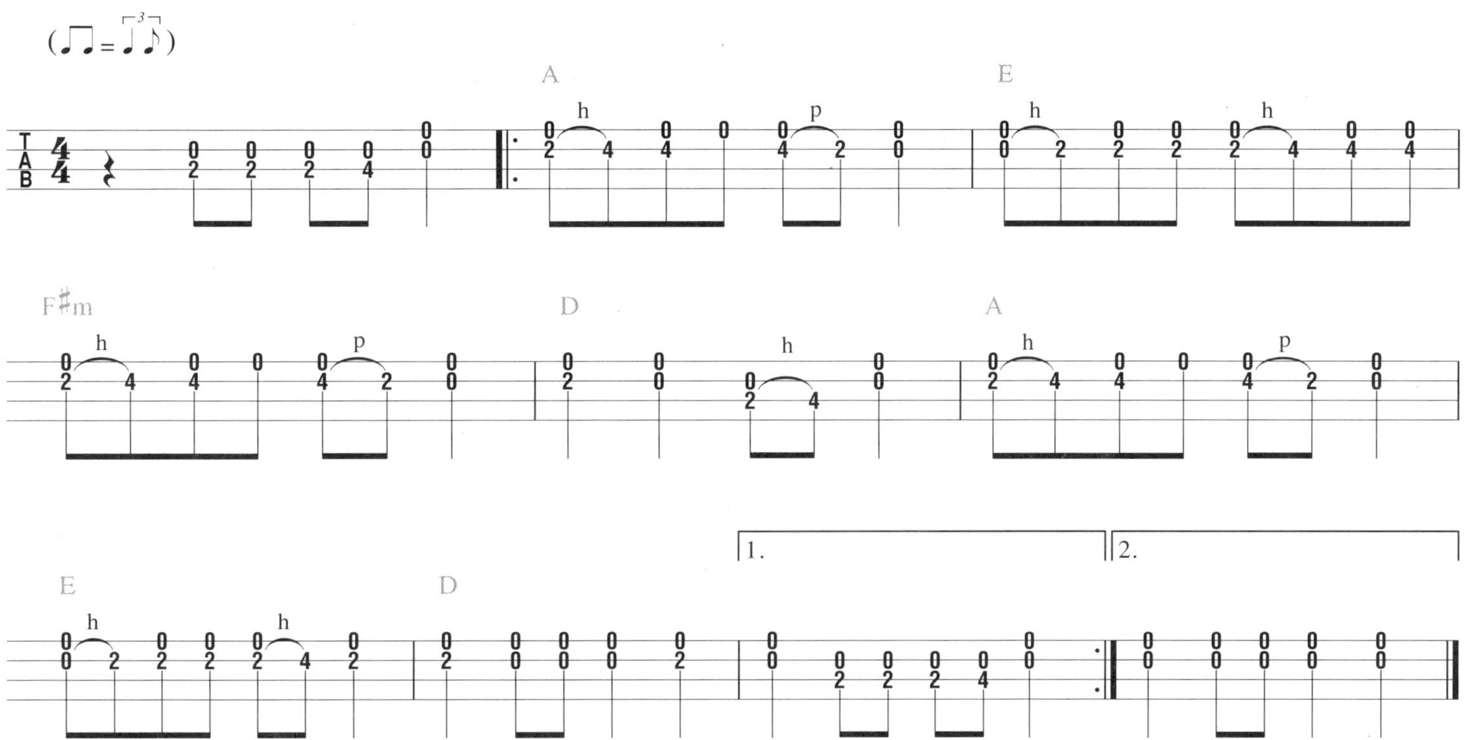

In "Eighth of January," we'll use a swing feel again. With two separate sections featuring first and second endings, be sure to return to the correct forward-facing repeat sign when you reach the backwards-facing one. (If you need a refresher, revisit the section on first and second endings in chapter 5.) Master this first solo before trying to tackle the more complex second solo.

EIGHTH OF JANUARY

Solo 1

Traditional

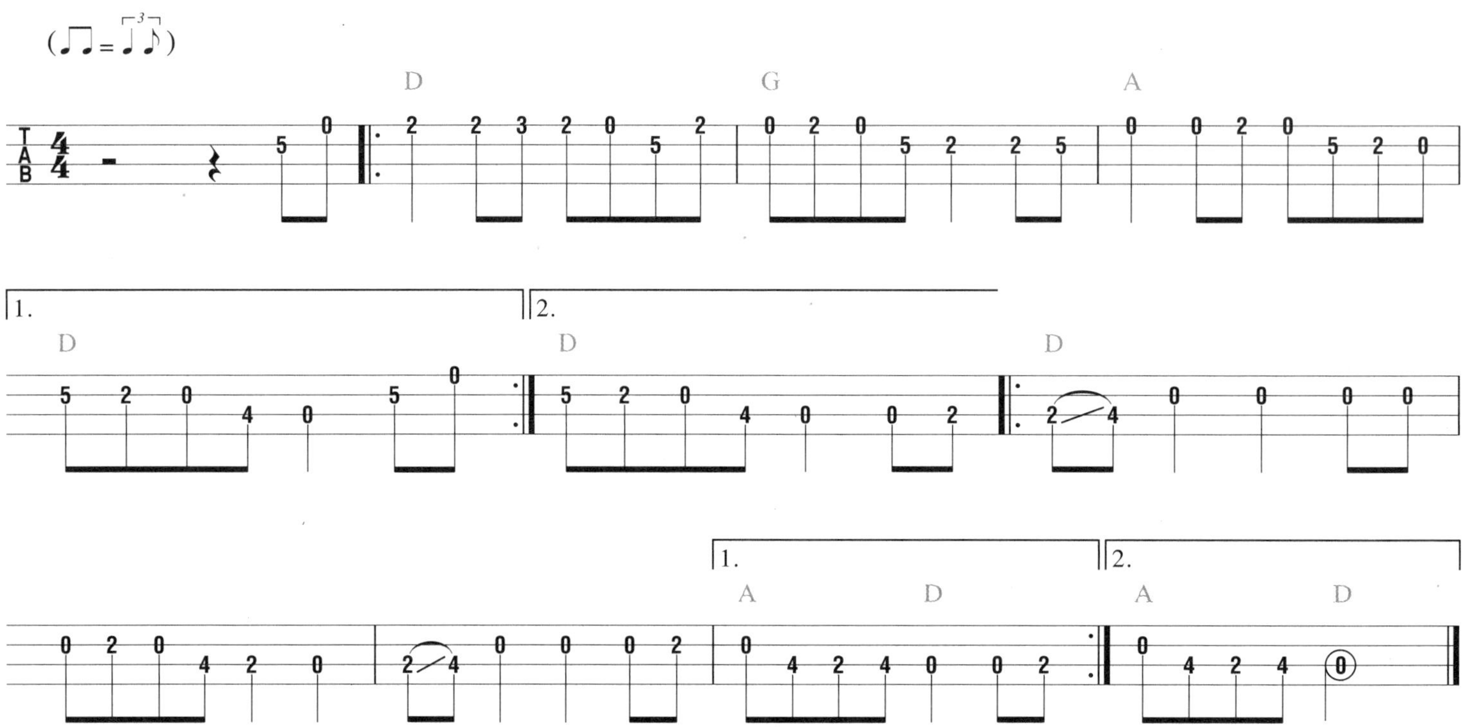

In the second version of "Eighth of January," the pickup notes start on beat "3-and," so you'll start the song with an upstroke of your pick on the upbeat right after beat 3. To account for the silent downbeat right before this note, you're going to see a new type of rest in the music called an *eighth rest*, which has the same value as an eighth note.

To keep things interesting, we're also going to try out a few new ways to play hammer-ons, pull-offs, and slides. In measures 2 and 3, you may notice that the pull-offs begin on "and" beats. This means that the second note of these eighth-note pull-offs naturally fall on downbeats, and since these notes aren't plucked with your pick, you'll end up playing two upstrokes in a row.

Skip ahead to the slides at the beginning of measures 6 and 8 (we don't count the pick-up measure when numbering measures) and notice that the two notes used in this slide are sixteenth notes, not eighth notes or quarter notes. Since two sixteenth notes fill the same time as one eighth note, you'll use a downstroke on the 2nd fret of the D string and slide up to the 4th fret—all on the downbeat. Then continue on to the next note as usual, using an upstroke on the open A string on the "and" count. As mentioned in chapter 2, it can help to count "**1**-e-&-a, **2**-e-&-a, **3**-e-&-a, **4**-e-&-a" for the sixteenth notes, with each syllable representing one sixteenth note.

Lastly, in measures 7 and 9, we're going to play a combo hammer-on/pull-off using just one downstroke. Start with your first finger on the 2nd fret and pluck the string; then, use your second finger for the hammer-on to the 4th fret; finally, pull the second finger back off to reveal the first finger, which should still be holding down the 2nd fret. Keep in mind that this all occurs on a single beat! We're using two sixteenth notes in the hammer-on, while the pull-off ends with an eighth note. To play the note on the next beat, simply follow the hammer-on/pull-off with another downstroke.

EIGHTH OF JANUARY

Solo 2

Traditional

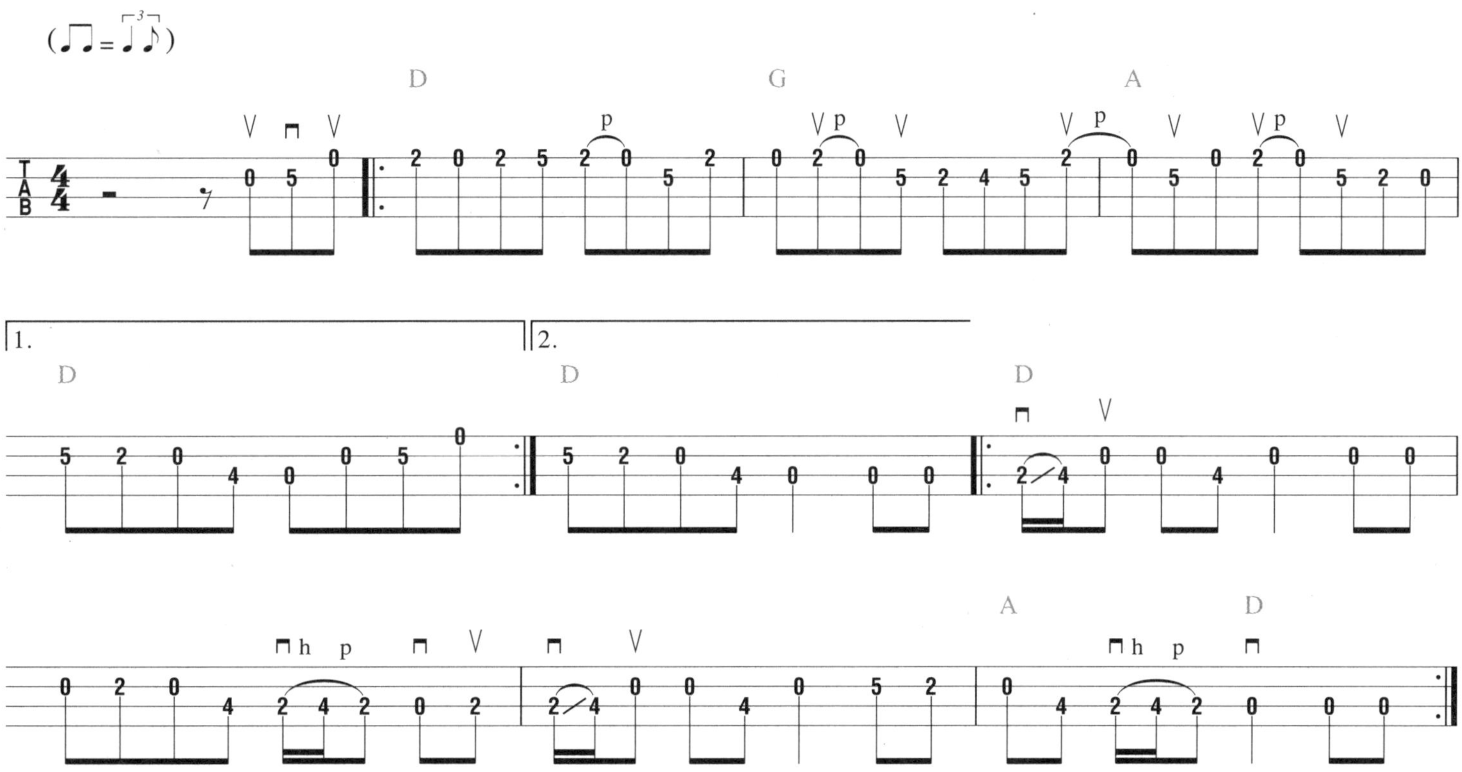

"Salt Creek" is another common fiddle tune you'll come across in a jam session. It's fun to play on the mandolin, as the B part is played higher up the neck, shifting between two different hand positions in measures 9–14. Be sure to follow the fingerings shown above the staff to correctly fret the notes higher up on the fretboard.

SALT CREEK

Solo 1

Traditional

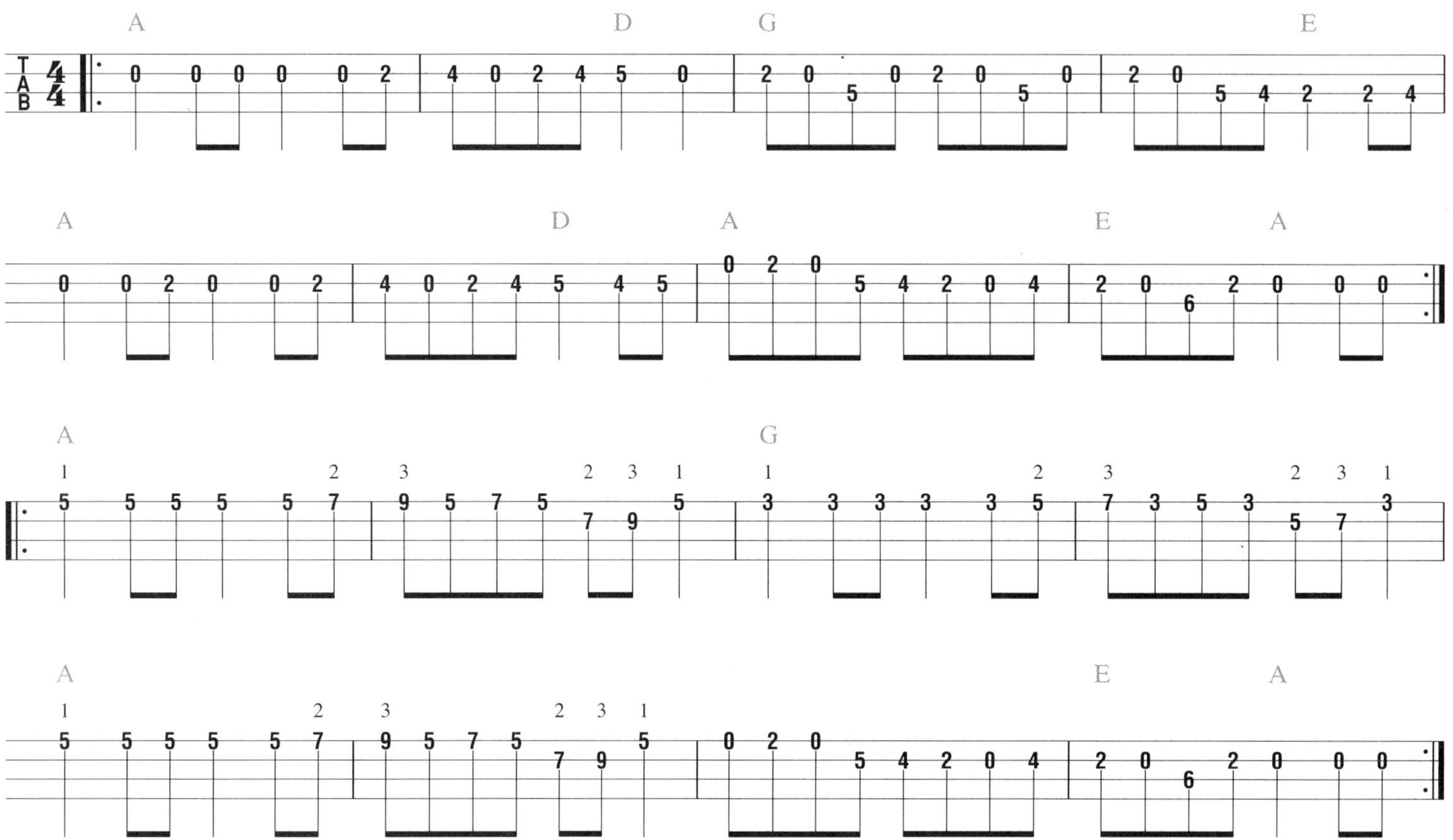

TOOLBOX

Positions

Early on in the book, I suggested that we should think of each fret-hand finger as being responsible for two frets: your first finger covers the 1st and 2nd frets, second finger is used on 3rd and 4th frets, third finger handles the 5th and 6th frets, and fourth finger manages the 7th fret. When your hand is in this position, you're playing in what's called *first position*. If you shift everything up the neck two frets—with your first finger now responsible for the 3rd and 4th frets, second finger on the 5th and 6th frets, third finger on the 7th and 8th frets, and fourth finger on the 9th fret—you are now playing in *second position*. If you start the same pattern on the 5th and 6th frets, you're playing in *third position*. Lastly, if you need to play in *fourth position*, your hand would be positioned on the neck with your first finger on 7th and 8th frets, second on the 9th and 10th, and so on.

SALT CREEK

Solo 2

Traditional

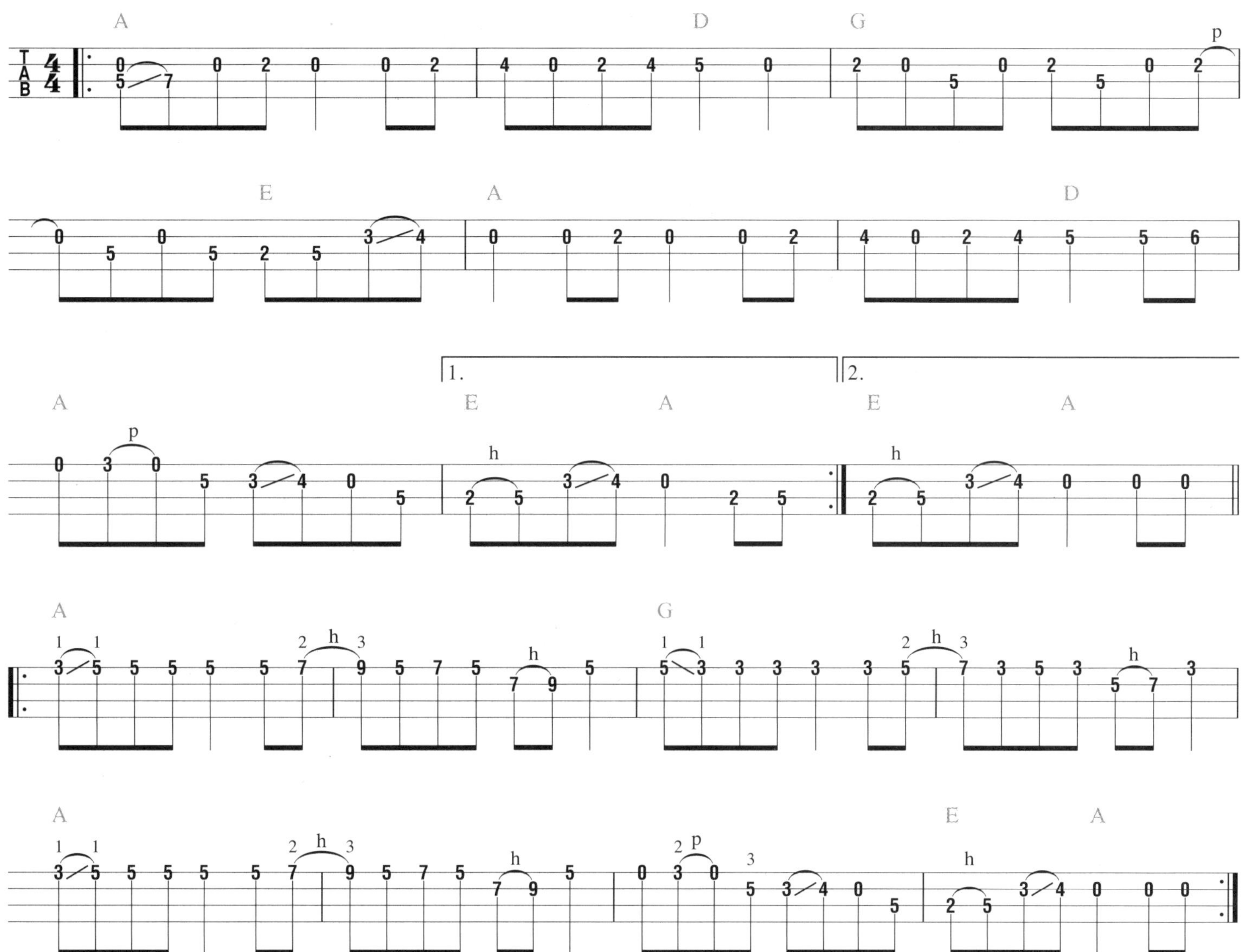

Chapter 8: Three- and Four-Finger Bluegrass Chords

By now, you should have developed enough strength in your fret-hand fingers to add a third and maybe fourth finger to the bluegrass chords you've been playing. For the three- and four-finger chords we're about to learn, it may still take you some time to be able to play each of the notes cleanly without any of the other fingers muting one or two of the strings.

To create a three-finger bluegrass chord, you can simply add your third finger to the chords you already know. As you see in the following chord frame, the three-finger G chord is made by placing your first finger on the 2nd fret of the A string, second finger on the 3rd fret of the E string, and third finger on the 5th fret of the D string. You can add your third finger to all of the basic bluegrass chords the same way: you'll always place your third finger on the next open string and skip one fret. One of the biggest stretches for your fingers will be the Gm chord, where you need to pull your first finger back to the 1st fret, as shown in the second chord frame.

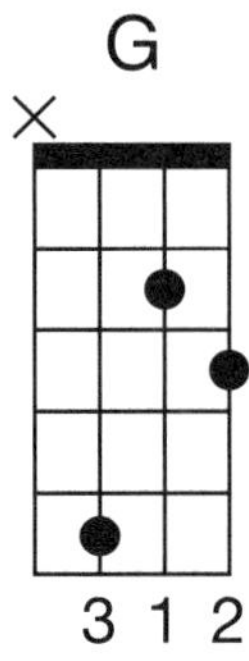

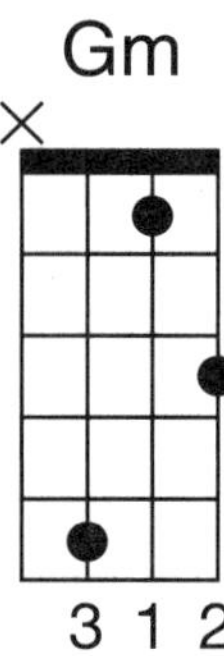

Once you have the three-finger chord shape down, you can add the fourth finger to the G string, skipping a fret this time, too. In the case of the G and Gm chords, you'll be adding it to the 7th fret of the G string. You are now able to strum (or chop) all four strings in all positions up and down the neck!

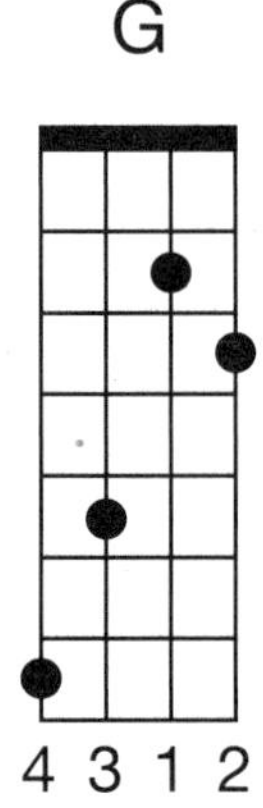

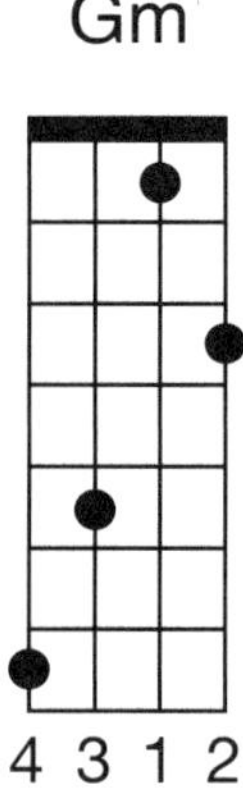

TOOLBOX

Tips & Tricks for Three- and Four-Finger Bluegrass Chords

These chord shapes can be easier to play where the frets are closer together, so I recommend practicing them further up the neck. Instead of starting with the G chord, try using the C chord with your middle finger on the 8th fret of the E string. (**Note:** This C chord is included in appendix C.) Once the C chord feels comfortable, move back towards the nut, one fret at a time, until you return to the G chord. Try this method with the minor shape, too. You'll know you've made good progress once you can cleanly play and hear every note of the four-finger Gm bluegrass chord.

Barre Chords

Though not often used in the "chop" rhythm of bluegrass music, *barre chords* (pronounced "bar chords") are commonly used in other styles of music, and they can be modified easily to create different "chord voicings" (more on this in chapter 11). To play a barre chord, you'll need to lay a flat first finger across some or all of the strings. These chords, for the most part, sound better when allowed to sustain, and they work well with a more "strummy" style of rhythm playing, similar to what a guitarist might do.

If you're already used to playing the two-, three-, and four-finger chop chords, you can start building your barre chords around the same two frets that your first and second fingers were on for those chords. This time, however, your fourth finger will fret the root note on the E string, and your third finger frets the A string. You then skip one fret back, towards the nut, and use your first finger to cover the remaining open strings with a *barre*, meaning your first finger is laid flat across the strings at the same fret, as indicated in the following chord frames with a curved line above the dots on the same fret. Here are the different major and minor barre-chord shapes, depending on whether the root note is on the E string or the A string. (**Note**: We're going to call the three-note version of this chord shape—with the root note on the A string—a barre chord, even though, technically, it doesn't include a barre; it's the same basic shape, but we'd need another string beyond the G string to complete the barre; the E string should not be played at all when the root of this barre chord shape is on the A string.)

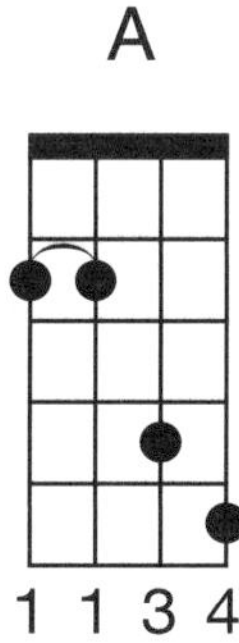

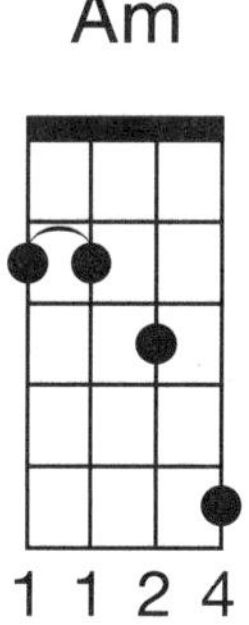

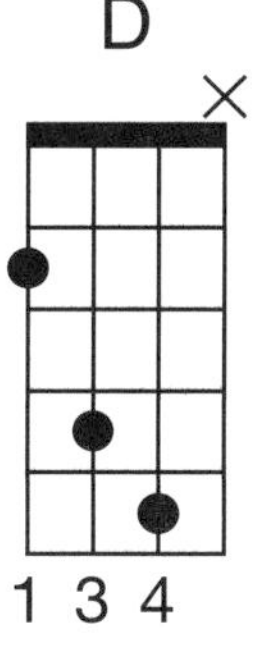

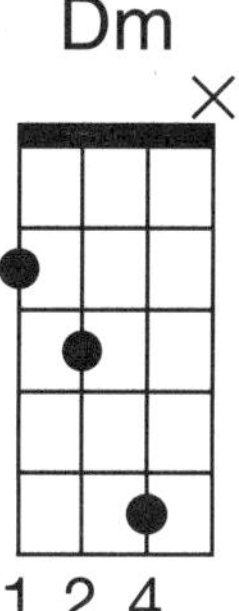

Let's try a few songs using barre chords. Use the Note Finder in the appendix to find the correct root note to build these barre chords on. (**Note**: You can also find the chord frames for the barre chords used in the following songs in the appendix, but it's good practice to try building them on your own first by using what you just learned.)

ELEANOR RIGBY

Words and Music by John Lennon and Paul McCartney

C *(2 m.)* **Em** *(2 m.)* **C** *(2 m.)* **Em** *(2 m.)*
Ah, look at all the lonely people! Ah, look at all the lonely people!

Verse

Em *(3 m.)* **C** *(1 m.)*
Eleanor Rigby picks up the rice in the church where a wedding has been,

C *(1/2 m.)* **Em** *(1 m.)*
Lives in a dream.

Em *(2 1/2 m.)* **C** *(1 m.)*
Waits at the window, wearing the face that she keeps in a jar by the door,

C *(1/2 m.)* **Em** *(1/2 m.)*
Who is it for?

Chorus

Em *(2 m.)* **C** *(1 m.)* **Em** *(1 m.)*
All the lonely people, where do they all come from?

Em *(2 m.)* **C** *(1 m.)* **Em** *(1 m.)*
All the lonely people, where do they all belong?

LOSING MY RELIGION

Words and Music by William Berry, Peter Buck, Michael Mills and Michael Stipe

Am *(2 m.)* **Em** *(2 m.)* **Am** *(2 m.)*
Oh, life is bigger. It's bigger than you, and you are not me.

Em *(2 m.)* **Am** *(2 m.)*
The lengths that I will go to, the distance in your eyes.

Em *(2 m.)* **Dm** *(2 m.)* **G** *(2 m.)*
Oh no, I've said too much. I set it up.

Am *(2 m.)* **Em** *(2 m.)* **Am** *(2 m.)*
That's me in the corner. That's me in the spotlight, losing my religion,

Em *(2 m.)* **Am** *(2 m.)*
Trying to keep up with you, and I don't know if I can do it.

Em *(2 m.)* **Dm** *(2 m.)* **G** *(2 m.)*
Oh no, I've said too much. I haven't said enough.

F *(2 m.)* **Am** *(2 m.)*
I thought that I heard you laughing. I thought that I heard you sing.

F *(2 m.)* **Am** *(2 m.)*
I think I thought I saw you try.

Chapter 9:
3/4 Time & Tremolo

So far, all of the songs that we've played have been in 4/4 time, which means that there are four beats per measure and each beat is equivalent to one quarter note. The next most common time signature in bluegrass and folk music is 3/4 time, sometimes called waltz time. In 3/4 time, there are three beats per measure and, again, each beat is equal to one quarter note. We count it as **1**-2-3, **1**-2-3... emphasizing the first beat of each measure. When playing a basic rhythm in 3/4 time on the mandolin, we strum on beats 2 and 3. Think of a waltz dancer (pause-step-step, pause-step-step) and you'll get it right (pause-strum-strum, pause-strum-strum).

Let's try using 3/4 time in a few songs. In the final measure of "Amazing Grace," you'll see a circled note with a dot next to it. This type of note is known as a *dotted half note*. When we add a dot to any note value, we add half of that note's value to the duration. So, a dotted half note is always worth three beats—pretty useful in 3/4 time!

AMAZING GRACE

Words by John Newton
Traditional American Melody

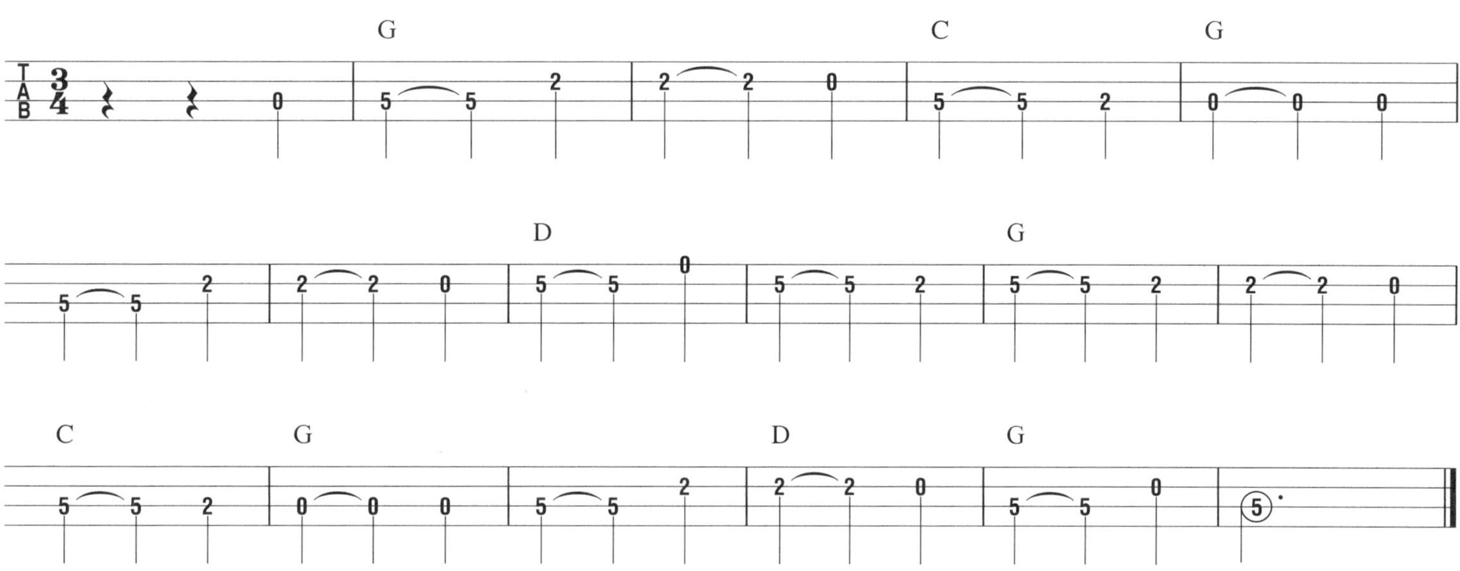

In the next version of "Amazing Grace," play through the solo melody first, and then go back and play the chords, as demonstrated in the audio.

AMAZING GRACE

Solo & Chords

Words by John Newton
Traditional American Melody

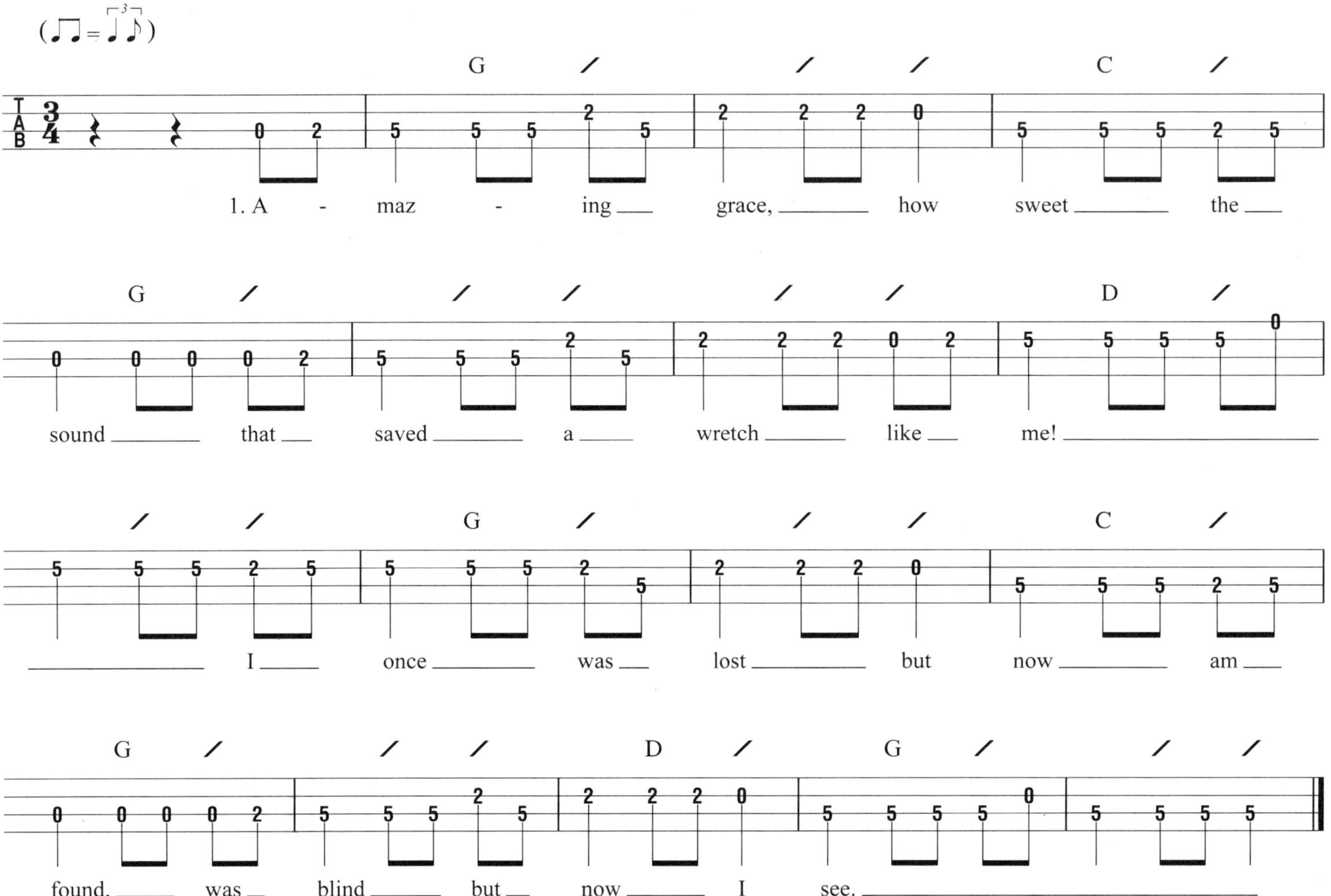

TOOLBOX

Tremolo

Tremolo is a very common technique used on the mandolin. It's a way of sustaining long notes that would otherwise fade quickly if you only plucked the note once. Tremolo is accomplished by playing rapid downstrokes and upstrokes with a pick on the same note, and it's notated in music by placing three diagonal lines across the stem of a note. Tremolo can be played on a single set of strings or on multiple strings. When playing tremolo, you want to keep an evenly spaced, rapid succession of downstrokes and upstrokes until that note ends.

In the first solo of "Amazing Grace" that we looked at, we held two tied quarter notes over the first two beats of almost every measure. Now, let's try adding tremolo to these notes to help them stand out better.

AMAZING GRACE

Tremolo

Words by John Newton
Traditional American Melody

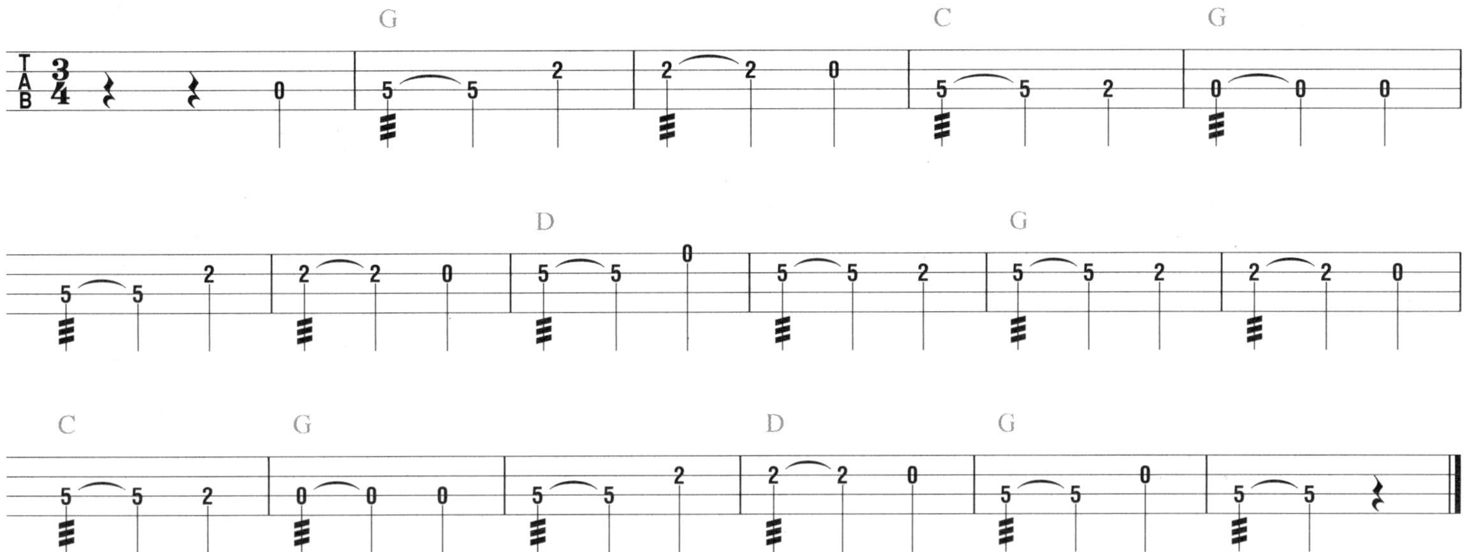

The next version of "Amazing Grace" includes tremolo over double-stops. Watch the accompanying video for a demonstration of how to use tremolo when playing double-stops.

AMAZING GRACE

Tremolo with Double-stops

Words by John Newton
Traditional American Melody

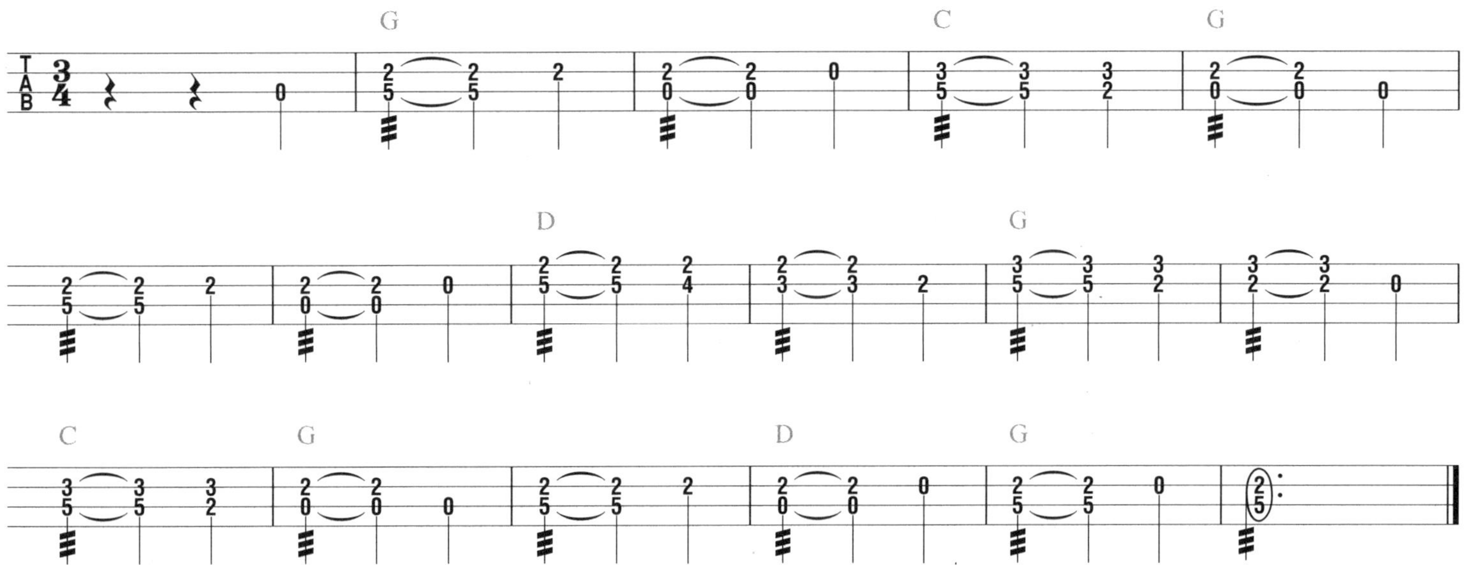

We'll finish out this chapter with two more songs that include tremolo and double-stops.

ASHOKAN FAREWELL

Tremolo with Double-stops

Theme from PBS Series THE CIVIL WAR

By Jay Ungar

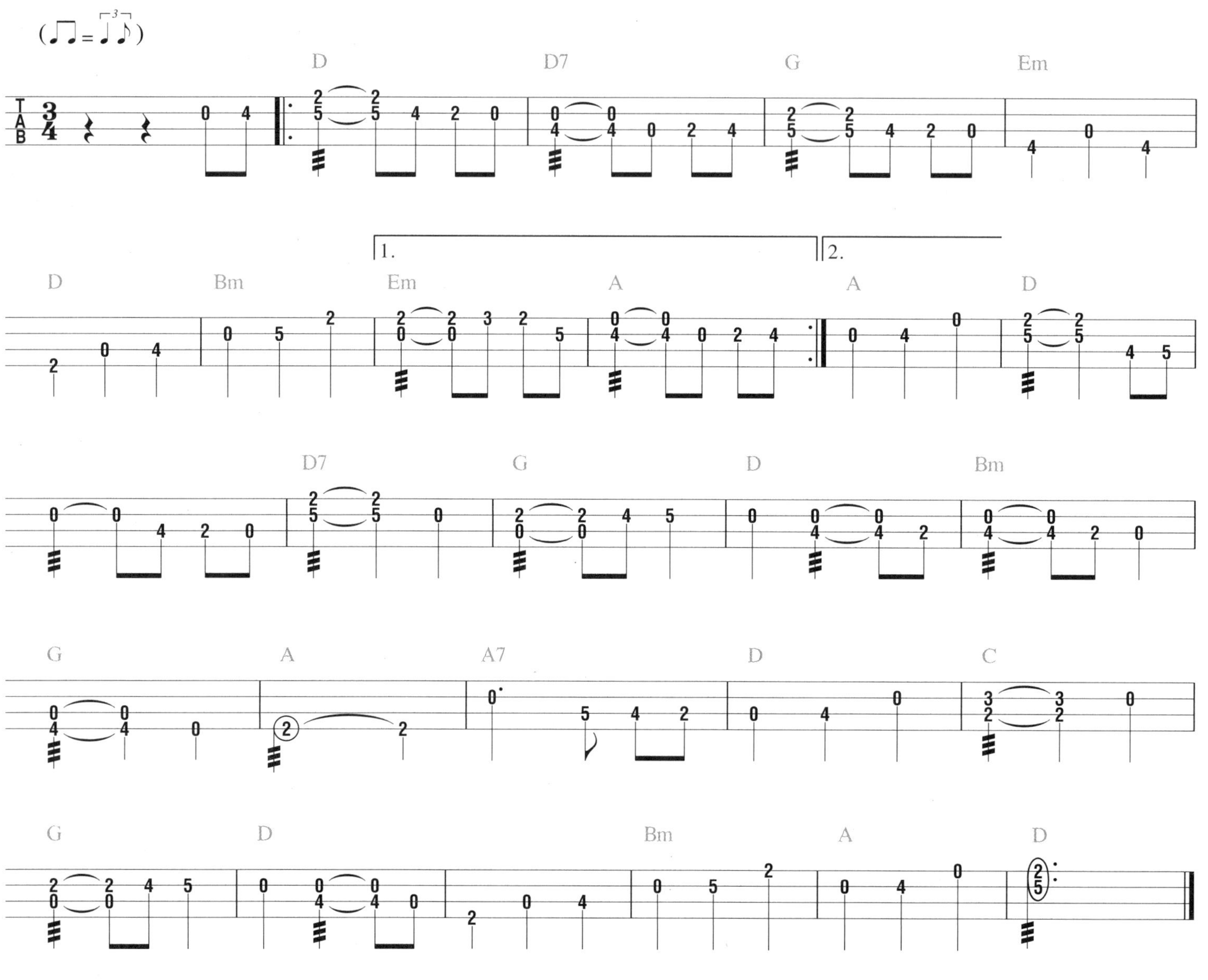

Watch the accompanying video for a demonstration of the next song. It might be a challenge for you at this point to hold down the 1st fret on the E string while also sliding from the 3rd fret to the 5th fret on the A string, so it's something you might want to practice on its own.

LONESOME MOONLIGHT WALTZ

Tremolo with Double-stops

By Bill Monroe

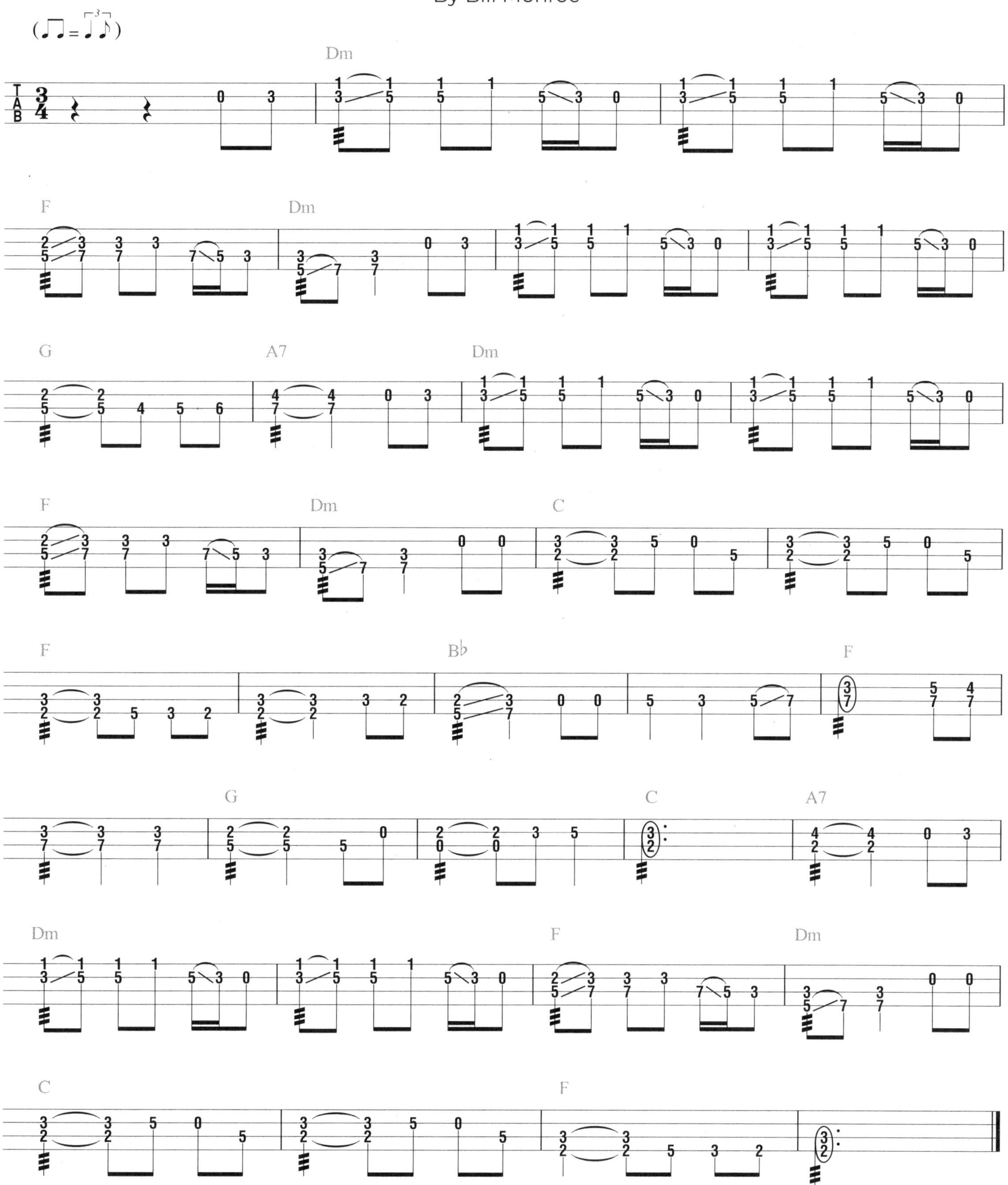

Chapter 10:
Closed Position

We have the ability to move solos anywhere on the mandolin fretboard, allowing us to transpose to any other key. In order to do this, we have to learn to play the solo in a position higher up the fretboard, and any open notes in the solo will now be moved up to become fretted notes. When you're playing higher up the fretboard like this, you are in a *closed position*, and once you learn to do this, you'll be able to pick out melodies, change keys, and improvise easily. Let's go over how this works, and when and how to use it.

The key (no pun intended) to the closed position is to first put your first finger on the root note (the note that's the same name as the key you're playing in) and then follow the major scale pattern that we learned in chapter 2: skip a fret between each of your first three fingers (whole steps), then play the very next fret (half step) with your fourth finger, and finally repeat the same pattern one string higher. For help finding root notes on the fretboard, see the Note Finder in the appendix.

In the key of B, for example, we start with our first finger on the 2nd fret of the A string (our root B note). Then we skip to the 4th fret with our second finger, skip to the 6th fret with our third finger, and finish the string with our fourth finger on the 7th fret; we start over on the 2nd fret of the E string with our first finger, skip to the 4th with our second finger, 6th with our third finger, and finally end up with our fourth finger playing the B note one octave higher on the 7th fret.

As stated before, most songs in Western music can be played with only this pattern. When using the closed position, we can start this pattern on any note (making it our root note) to play in the key of that note, always using the same fingering. Watch the accompanying video to learn more. Then, when you're ready, let's go back to our nursery rhymes to get the hang of this new technique.

MARY HAD A LITTLE LAMB

Closed Position – Key of B

Words by Sarah Josepha Hale

Traditional Music

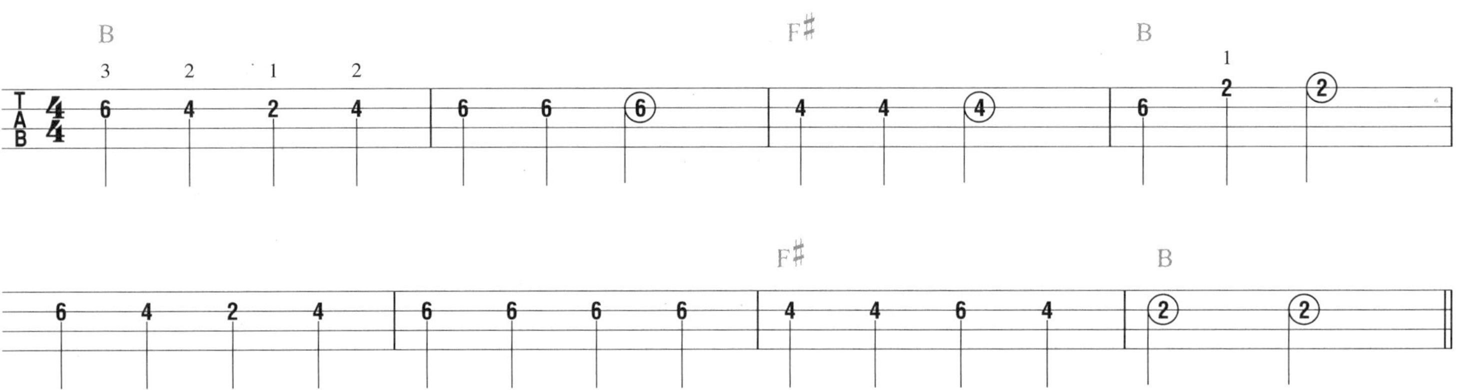

You'll recall from earlier that songs often don't start on the root note, but they will commonly resolve or end there. "Mary Had a Little Lamb" does end on the root B note, under our first finger, but it begins with our third finger on the third note of the scale—this note seems to be the second most common starting note, in my experience, so it's something to keep in mind when you're trying to figure out a melody by ear.

Since this melody is in closed position and there are no open strings included, we can reuse the same pattern to play the melody in any key we want. Let's try it in the key of G.

MARY HAD A LITTLE LAMB

Closed Position – Key of G

Words by Sarah Josepha Hale
Traditional Music

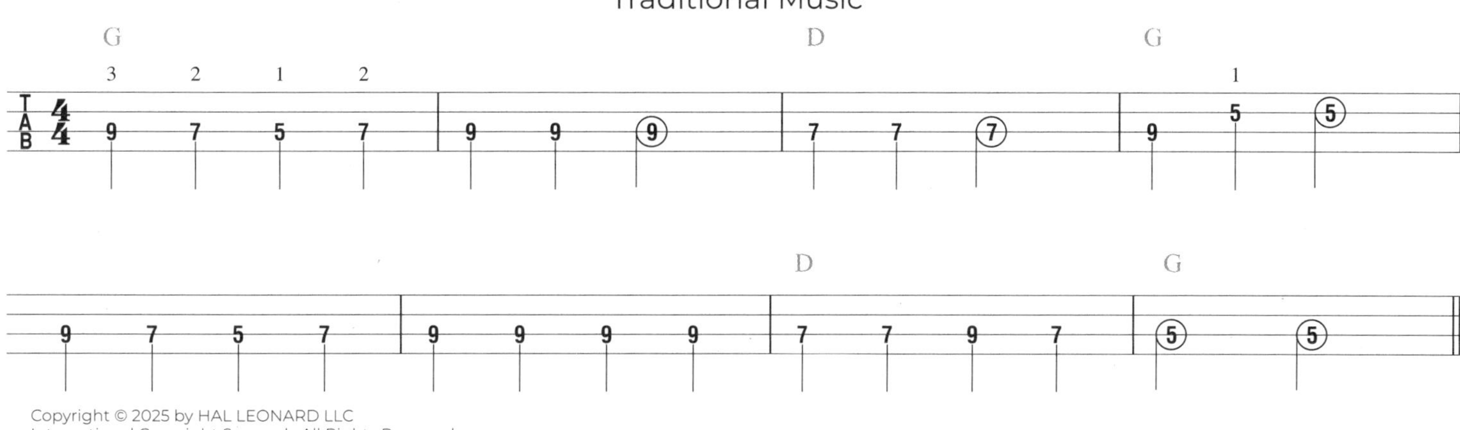

Seriously, try it anywhere on the neck. For example, place your first finger on the 8th fret of the A string. (This will be our root note, F, but it's not our starting note.) Then skip one fret between your first three fingers, placing your third finger on the 12th fret to find the starting note. Now you'll be in the right position to play this melody in the key of F (the pattern begins with frets 12, 10, 8, 10, 12, 12, 12...). When using the closed position, no key is more difficult to play in than any other!

Let's try this again with another melody we played earlier in the book.

TWINKLE, TWINKLE LITTLE STAR

Closed Position – Key of B

Traditional

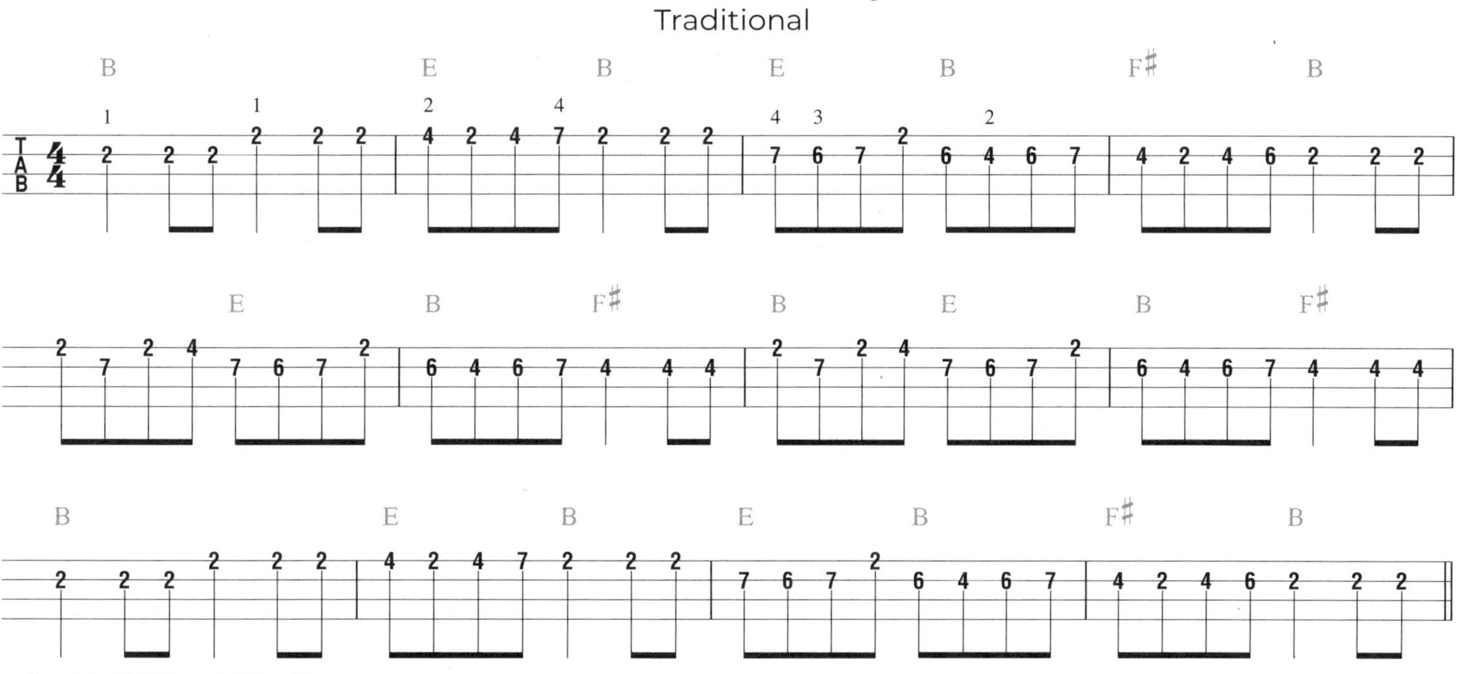

What's that, Uncle Joe? The key of B is too high for your voice? You would prefer E♭? OK!

TWINKLE, TWINKLE LITTLE STAR

Closed Position – Key of E♭

Traditional

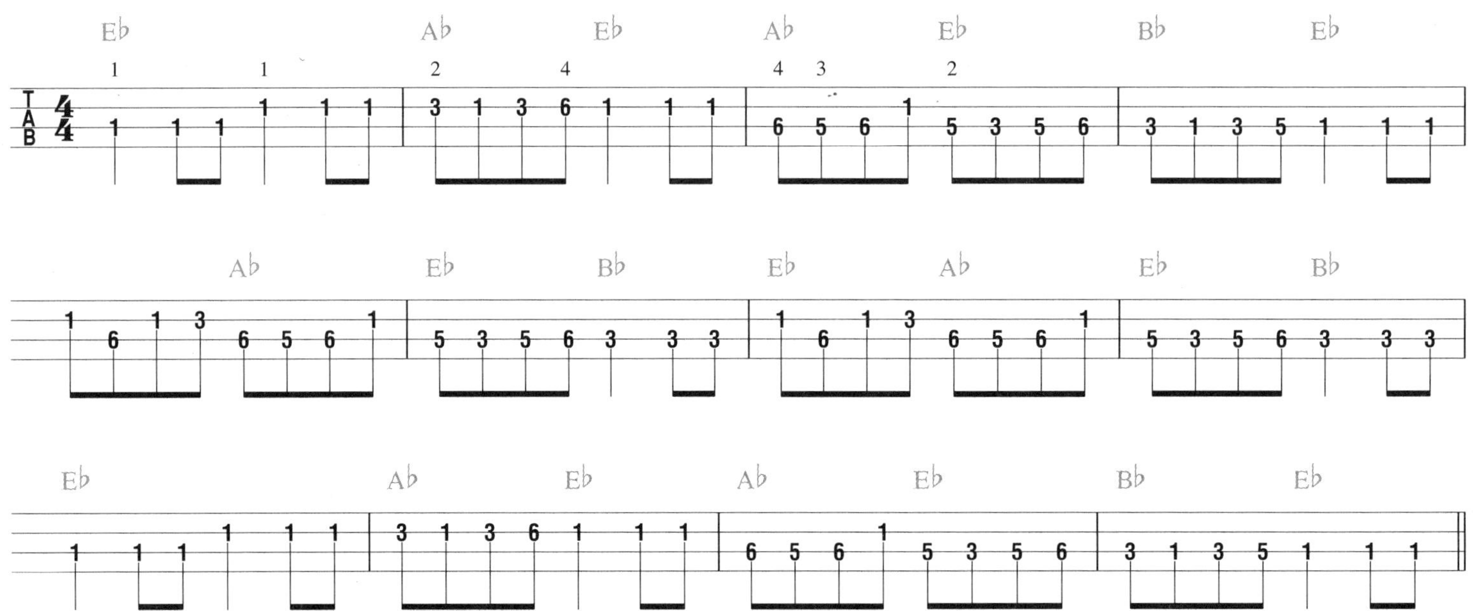

TOOLBOX

Using Closed Position with Singers

For the most part, fiddle tunes and instrumentals (songs with no singing) are written in keys that take advantage of the open strings (keys like D, A, G, C) and so we stay in that key when performing them. For example, there's no real need to learn "Salt Creek" in a closed position unless you just want the practice. However, everyone has a different vocal range when they sing, and while you may have learned a great solo to a song in the key of G, if some of the notes in the melody are too low for your lead singer (because they simply can't go that low), you'll need to put the closed position to use and move to a key that they're more comfortable in.

In "This Little Light of Mine," you'll need to temporarily go out of position to reach back and grab the 4th fret on the D string. Watch the accompanying video for tips on playing both of the following versions of this tune.

THIS LITTLE LIGHT OF MINE

Closed Position – Key of G

Traditional

There's another awesome bonus to playing in the closed position on the mandolin: it can help make a solo sound much more developed and fuller, because playing in a closed position allows you to add double-stops to any note. The correct double-stop notes aren't always available when using open notes, depending on the key you're playing in, but it's easy to find the double-stops in the closed position. Any note of the melody that's played using your second or third finger can be harmonized with your first finger, on the fret it usually plays in that position, on the next string higher. Let's try "This Little Light of Mine" again, but this time let's add the first finger to some of the notes to create double-stops.

THIS LITTLE LIGHT OF MINE

Closed Position with Double-stops

Traditional

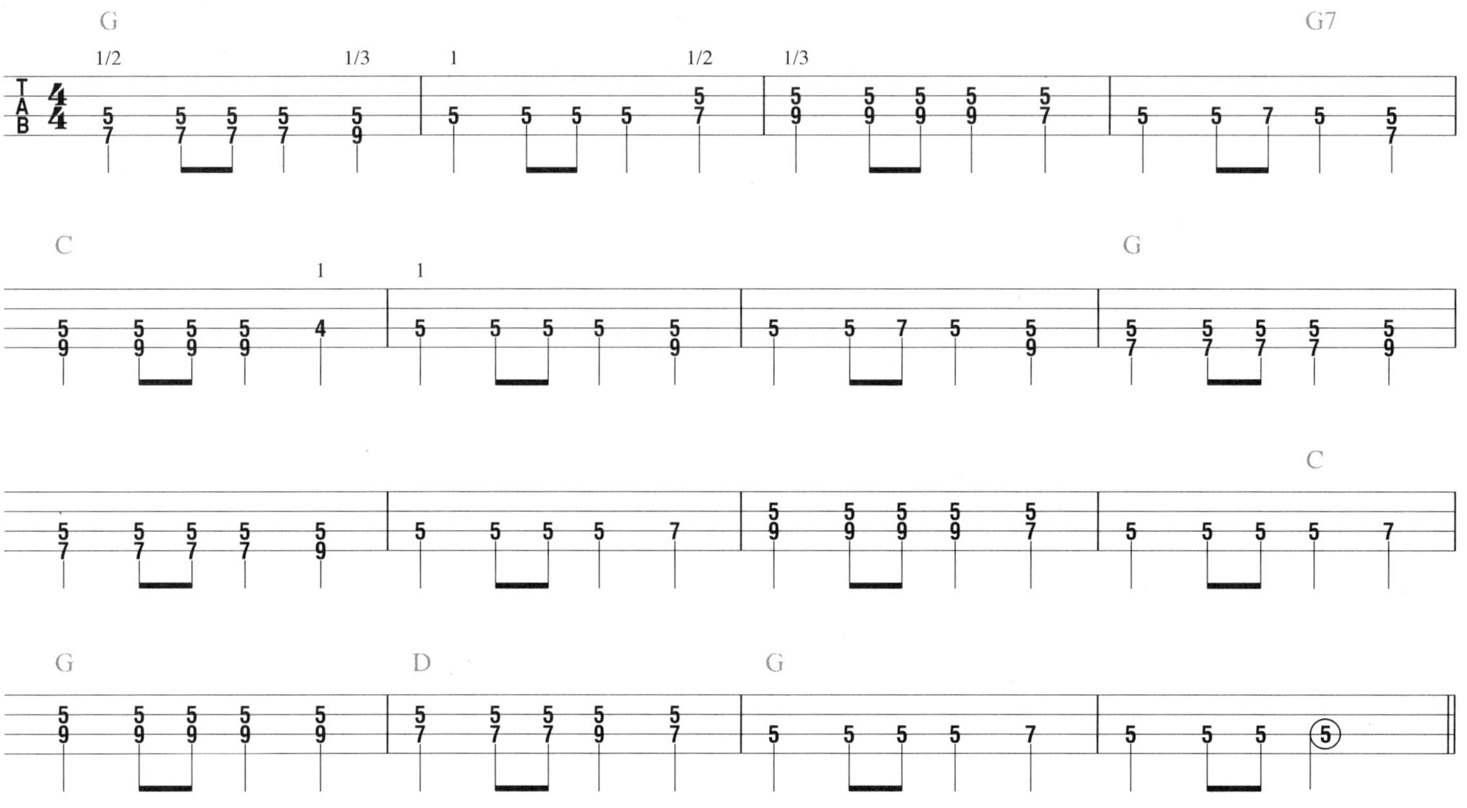

Over the years, I've found the starting note under your middle finger to be the most common starting note (as in "This Little Light of Mine"). This note is the fifth note of the scale, but since we're playing it below the root note (which is the 5th fret of the D string), not above, we refer to it as the "fifth below." To see this for yourself, start on the 5th fret of the D string and count up to the fifth note of the scale (frets 5, 7, 9, 10 on the D string, then fret 5 on the A string). If you drop that fifth note down one octave, you'll land on the "fifth below," which, again, is always located under your middle finger.

THE ANDY GRIFFITH SHOW THEME

(THE FISHIN' HOLE)

Closed Position – Key of C

By Earle Hagen and Herbert Spencer

Chapter 11: Chord Voicing

We create basic major chords by using the first, third, and fifth steps of a scale, and we can flat the third step to turn any major chord into a minor chord. One limitation to the mandolin having only four strings is in our ability to alter this standard 1-3-5 chord formation and add different notes to the chord. In chapter 8, I mentioned that barre chords are easy to modify to create new chords, so let's take a closer look at how chords, in general, are formed, and how barre chords can come in handy.

Chord Formation

A major chord is formed by playing the first (root), third, and fifth note of a scale together. The notes of the C major scale are C, D, E, F, G, A, and B (then the pattern starts all over again an octave up at C). If we play the first, third, and fifth notes of the scale (C, E, G) at the same time, they harmonize to make a C major chord. This note relationship is true in any key! For example, the notes of the A major scale are A, B, C#, D, E, F#, G#, (A), so playing the A, C#, and E together will give you an A major chord.

The three-finger bluegrass chop chords, such as our C chop chord, are kind of cheating. As we see with all other three-finger chop chords, the C chop chord doubles up the root note (5th fret, G string; 3rd fret, A string) and only adds the third note of the scale (2nd fret, D string). It's missing the fifth note of the scale, which technically makes it an incomplete chord. But since we do have the third note and the root note—and the third note isn't flat—we can still think of this as a major chord. (**Note**: Two notes played together are called a *dyad*, but it is OK to think of these as chords.) As you continue through this chapter, you'll learn how to create different types of more advanced chords, all built around our basic major or minor barre chord.

Using the A major barre chord as a template, we can work out some cool chord voicings for some very useful chord types that we don't know yet. Here, again, is the A major barre chord.

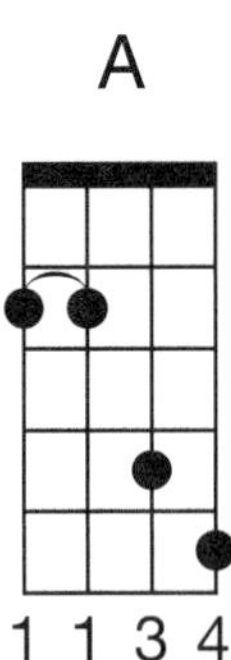

Before we start adjusting the chord, let's look a little more closely at each note in the A major chord. The notes played on the G String and the E string are both the root note (A). The note on the 2nd fret of the D string is the fifth note of the scale (E), and the 4th fret of the A string is the third note of the scale (C♯). Now, instead of calling the root note on the E string the first note of the scale, let's call it the eighth note of our scale. If we think of the note in this way, it makes it easy to see that we can make an Amaj7 chord (pronounced "A major seven" chord) by moving the eighth note down one fret so that the chord now includes the seventh note of the scale instead. (**Note**: Instead of using your fourth finger on the E string, you can instead try using a third-finger barre across the E and A strings.)

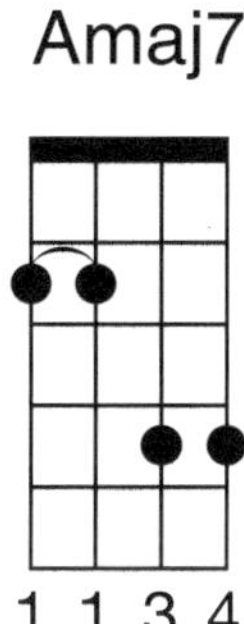

We can continue to move back one fret at a time on the E string. One more fret down gives us an A7 chord (pronounced "A seven" chord). Since the Amaj7 chord used the seventh note of the major scale, unaltered, we called it a "major 7" chord. This new A7 chord, also known as an A *dominant 7* chord, flats the seventh note.

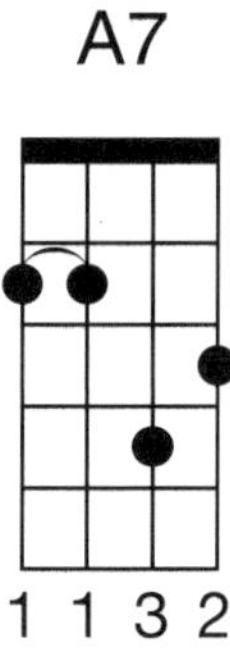

One more fret and we have an A6, which can be formed by using one of two fingerings. On the top string, we're now including the sixth note of the scale on top of the basic major chord.

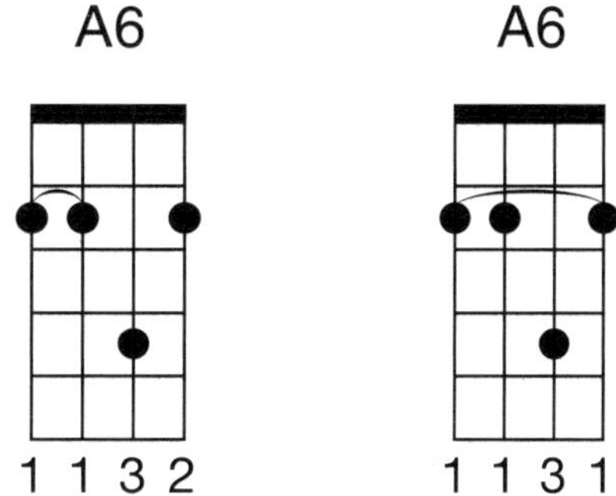

To turn any major barre chord into a minor barre chord, we flatten the third note of the scale used in the chord, as usual. For the A major chord, since the third note of the A major scale naturally includes a sharp (C♯), we simply remove the sharp to lower the note by a half step, giving us: A, C, E. After first lowering this note on the A string by one fret to create an Am barre chord, you can do the same thing that we just did with the major barre chord—moving the note on the E string down to create new chords. (**Note**: For the Am7 chord, you can either barre across the top two strings with your second finger, or you can use your second finger on the A string and your third finger on the E string, as shown.)

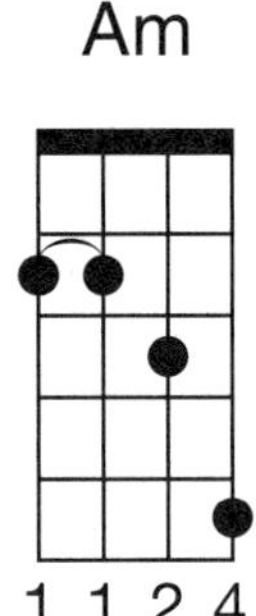

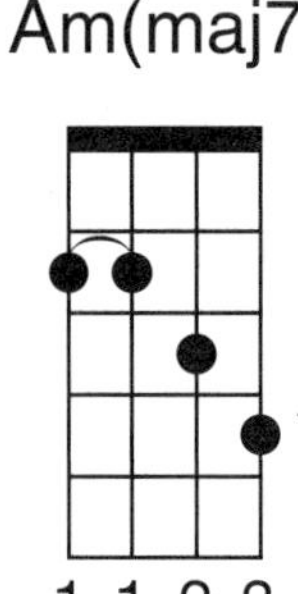

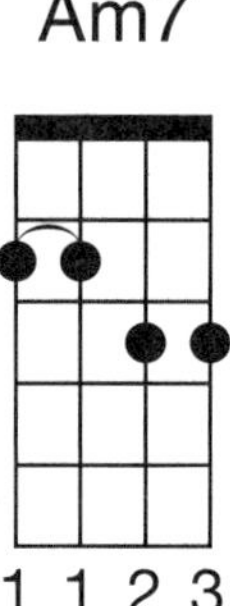

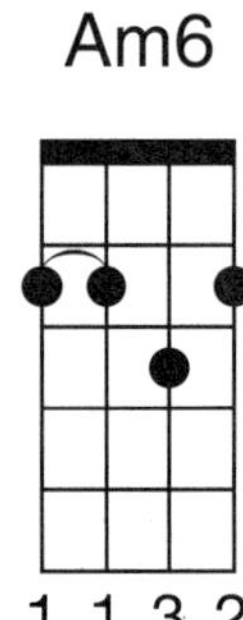

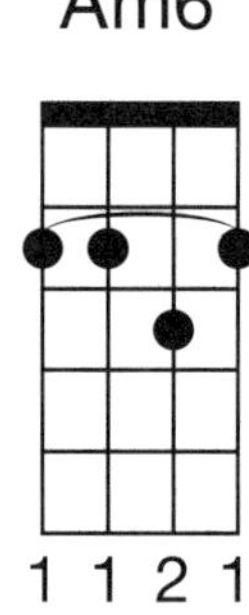

In the following two songs, we'll put a few of these new chord types to use. Use what you just learned in this lesson to form these chords; do this by referencing the Note Finder in appendix B to find the root note on the E string, and then build the appropriate chord shape upon that note.

GENTLE ON MY MIND

Words and Music by John Hartford

D *(1/2 m.)* **Dmaj7** *(1/2 m.)* **D6** *(1/2 m.)* **Dmaj7** *(1/2 m.)* **Em** *(2 m.)*
It's knowing that your door is always open and your path is free to walk

Em *(1/2 m.)* **Em(maj7)** *(1/2 m.)* **Em7** *(1/2 m.)* **A** *(1/2 m.)* **D** *(2 m.)*
That makes me tend to leave my sleeping bag rolled up and stashed behind your couch.

D *(1/2 m.)* **Dmaj7** *(1/2 m.)* **D6** *(1/2 m.)* **Dmaj7** *(1/2 m.)*
And it's knowing I'm not shackled by forgotten words and bonds

D *(1 m.)* **Em** *(2 m.)*
And the ink stains that have dried upon some line

Em *(1/2 m.)* **Em(maj7)** *(1/2 m.)* **Em7** *(1/2 m.)* **A** *(1/2 m.)*
That keeps you in the backroads by thew rivers of my mem'ry

Em *(1/2 m.)* **A** *(1/2 m.)* **D** *(1/2 m.)* **Dmaj7** *(1/2 m.)* **D6** *(1/2 m.)* **Dmaj7** *(1/2 m.)* **D**
That keeps you ever gentle on my mind.

TOOLBOX

Muting Unused Strings

When playing these shapes on just the lower three strings, try using part of your fretting hand to mute the top string. You don't want to actually fret the string, though; you just need to touch it with some part of your hand so that it won't ring out. By doing this, you'll be able to strum across all strings without worrying about playing a sour note.

In "Little Rock Getaway," we'll see a few *diminished seventh chords*, indicated by a small circle and the number "7." While this chord type is beyond the scope of this book, you can use the same chord shape for both diminished seventh chords, for now, to play along with the video. In the video, I play the melody first, then the strumming part. It's a fast-paced piece, so it may take you some time to match my tempo!

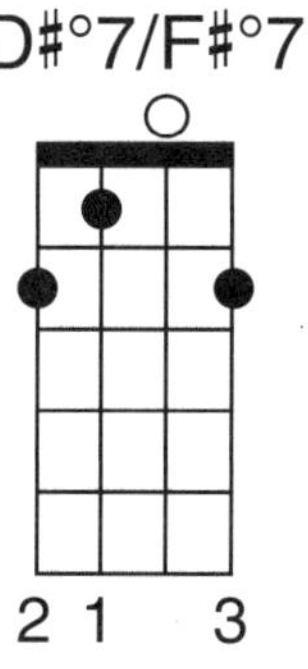

LITTLE ROCK GETAWAY

Music by Joe Sullivan
Words by Carl Sigman

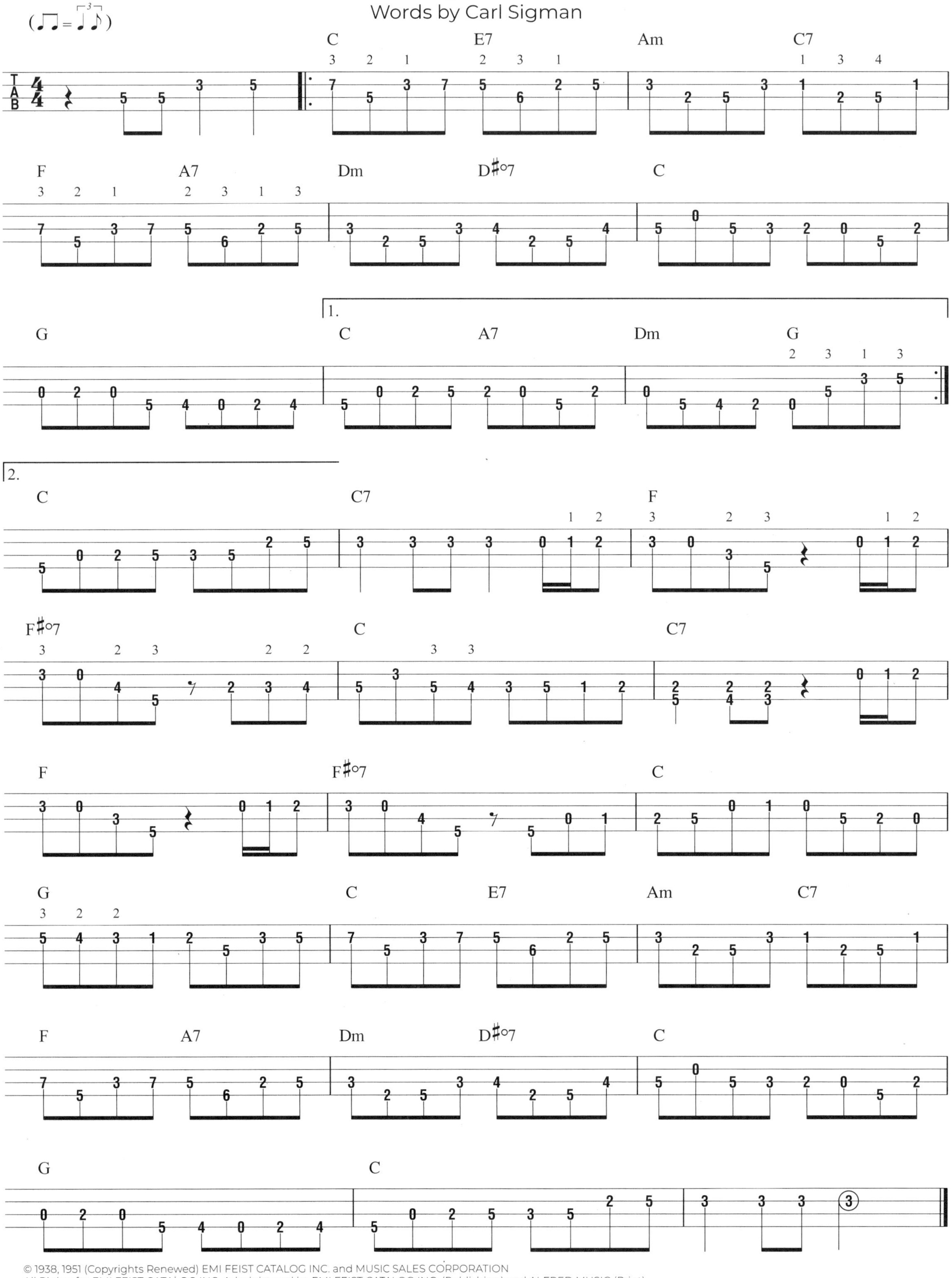

C E7 Am C7 F A7 Dm D♯°7 C G C A7 Dm G C C7 F F♯°7 C C7 F F♯°7 C G C E7 Am C7 F A7 Dm D♯°7 C G C

Chapter 12:
Cross-Picking

Cross-picking, a technique that sounds great on the mandolin, involves picking three or more strings in a repeated pattern. It's a lot like a banjo "roll," which uses three fingers to pick each string, but in our case, we'll use only a single flat pick. As with the banjo, there are a few picking patterns we can use to create a melody. The most common are the *forward roll*, which moves from the lowest string played to the highest (D, A, E, D, A, E...), and the *reverse roll*, which starts with the lowest string played and then works its way back from the highest string (D, E, A, D, E, A...). The *alternating roll* moves from lowest to highest and back again (D, A, E, A, D, A, E, A...).

To keep the correct number of beats per measure while playing a three-note pattern in 4/4 time, we often have to skip a string on the last beat to reset for the next measure (D, A, E, D, A, E, D, E / 1, &, 2, &, 3, &, 4, &). When we do this, we create a pattern that starts on the same note in each measure. Try the cross-picking technique for yourself in the following exercises and repeat each until the roll feels comfortable.

Cross-Picking – Forward Roll

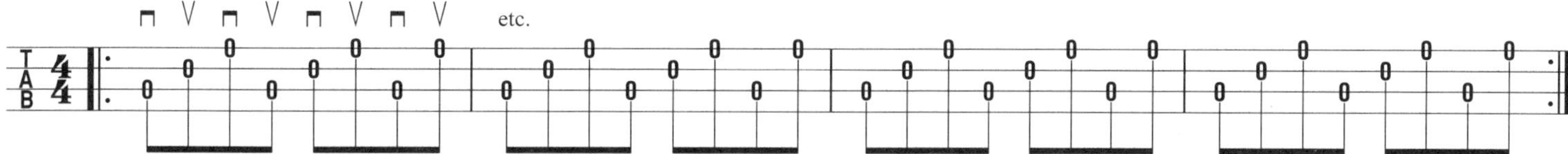

Cross-Picking – Reverse Roll

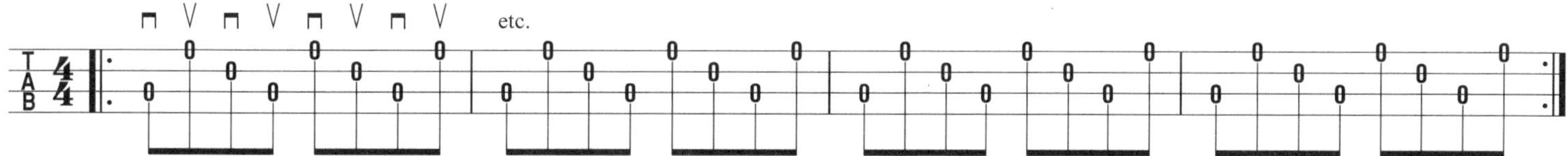

Cross-Picking – Alternating Roll

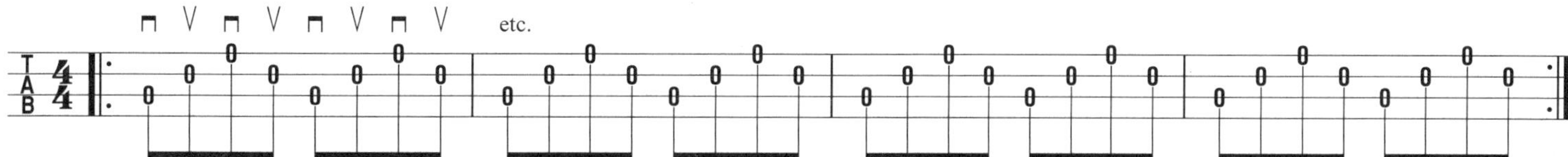

Now, let's try all of these cross-picking technique in a song.

BOIL THEM CABBAGE DOWN

Cross-Picking – Three Patterns

American Folksong

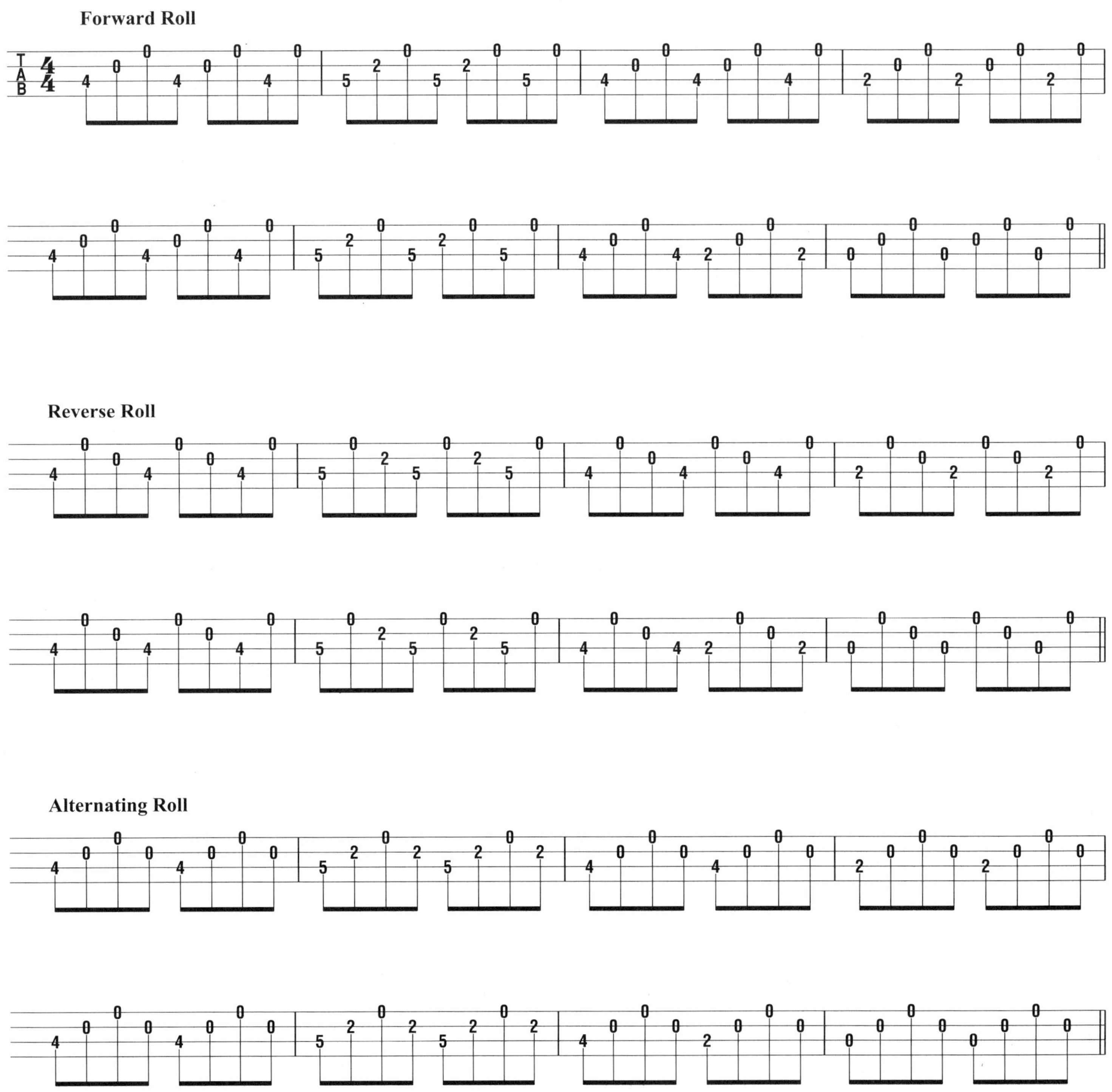

Watch the accompanying video for a demonstration of "Home Sweet Home." I'll play though it once at a slow tempo and then once at a faster speed.

HOME SWEET HOME

Cross-Picking

Words by John Howard Payne
Music by Henry R. Bishop

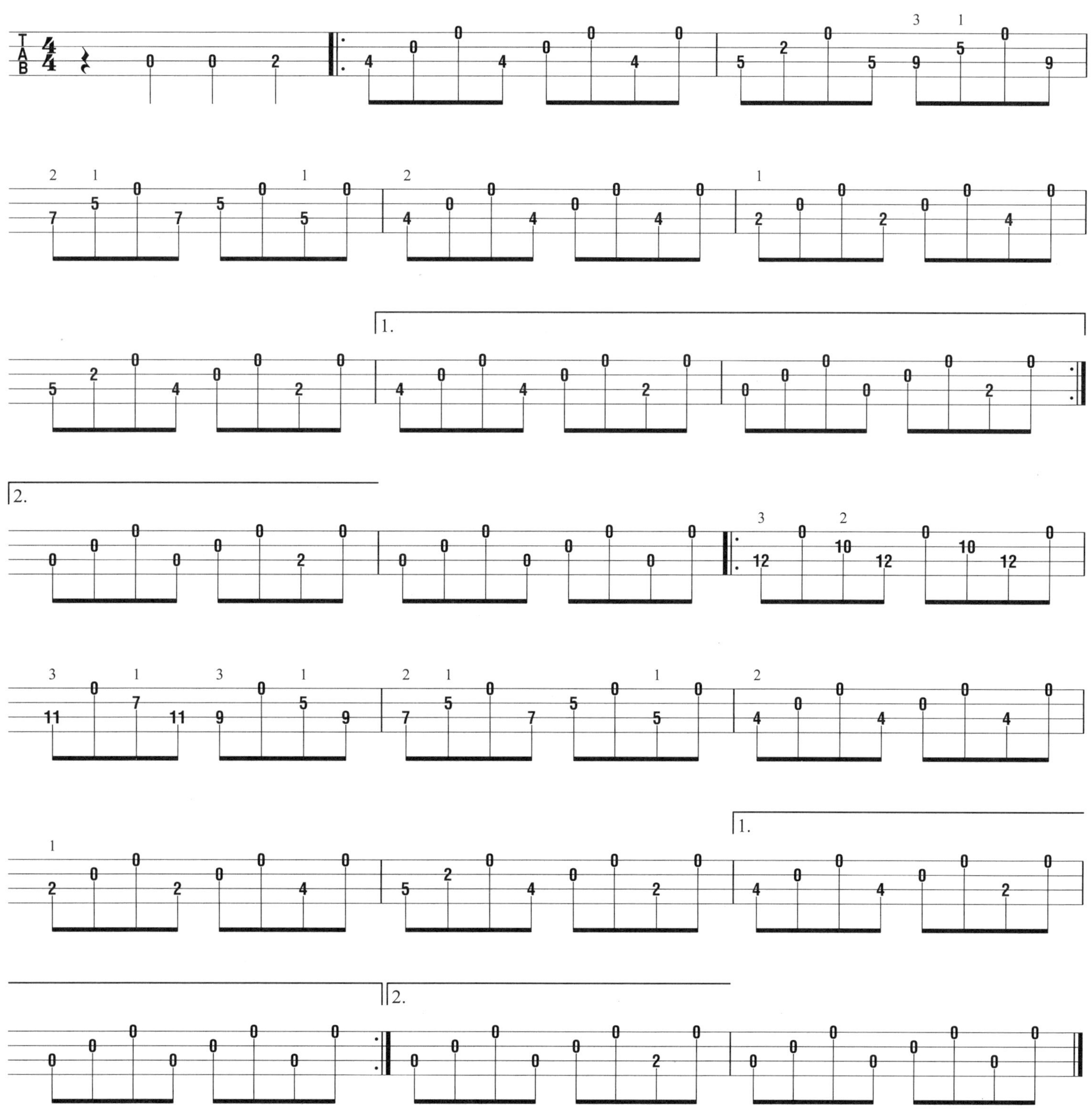

Chapter 13:

Celtic Music

Even though bluegrass music is now the style most synonymous with the mandolin, Bill Monroe, the "Father of Bluegrass," originally took inspiration from traditional Celtic and Scottish music. The mandolin makes a great addition to Celtic music—plus the fiddle parts used in the tunes can be a lot of fun to play. Here are a few of my favorites!

THE BOYS OF BLUEHILL

Traditional

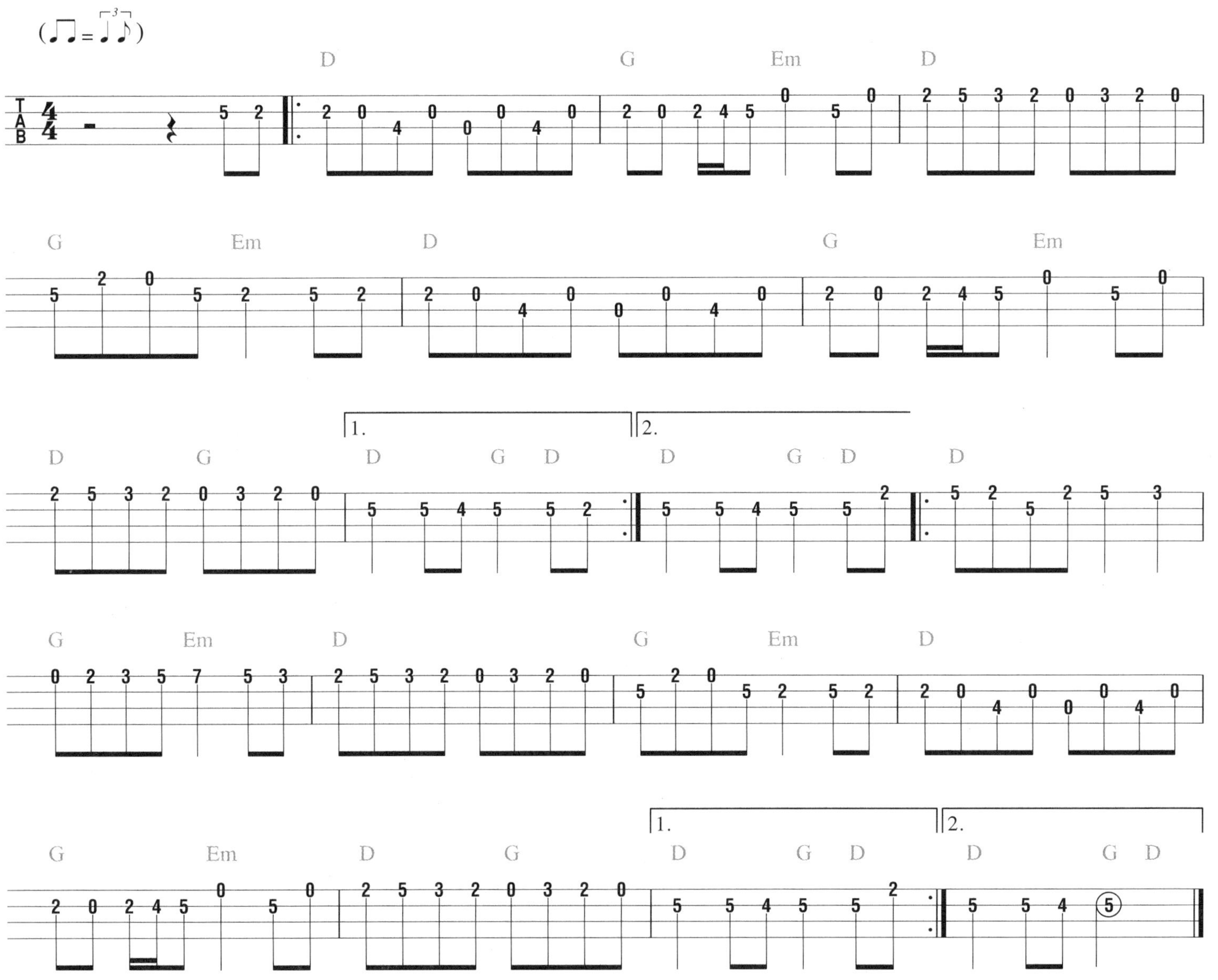

COOLEY'S REEL

Traditional Irish Folk Song

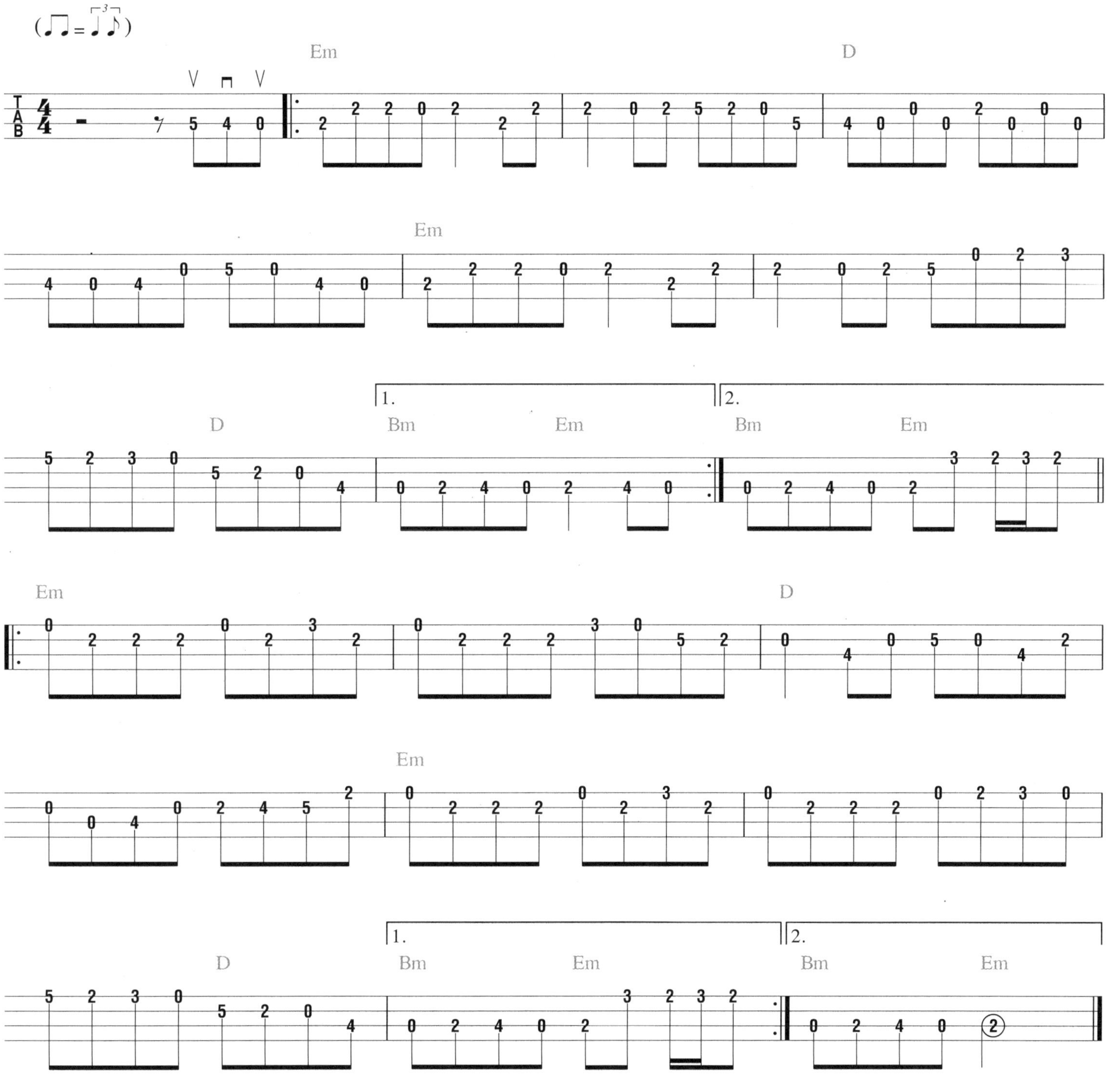

FATHER KELLY'S REEL

(The Rossmore Jetty)

By Father P.J. Kelly

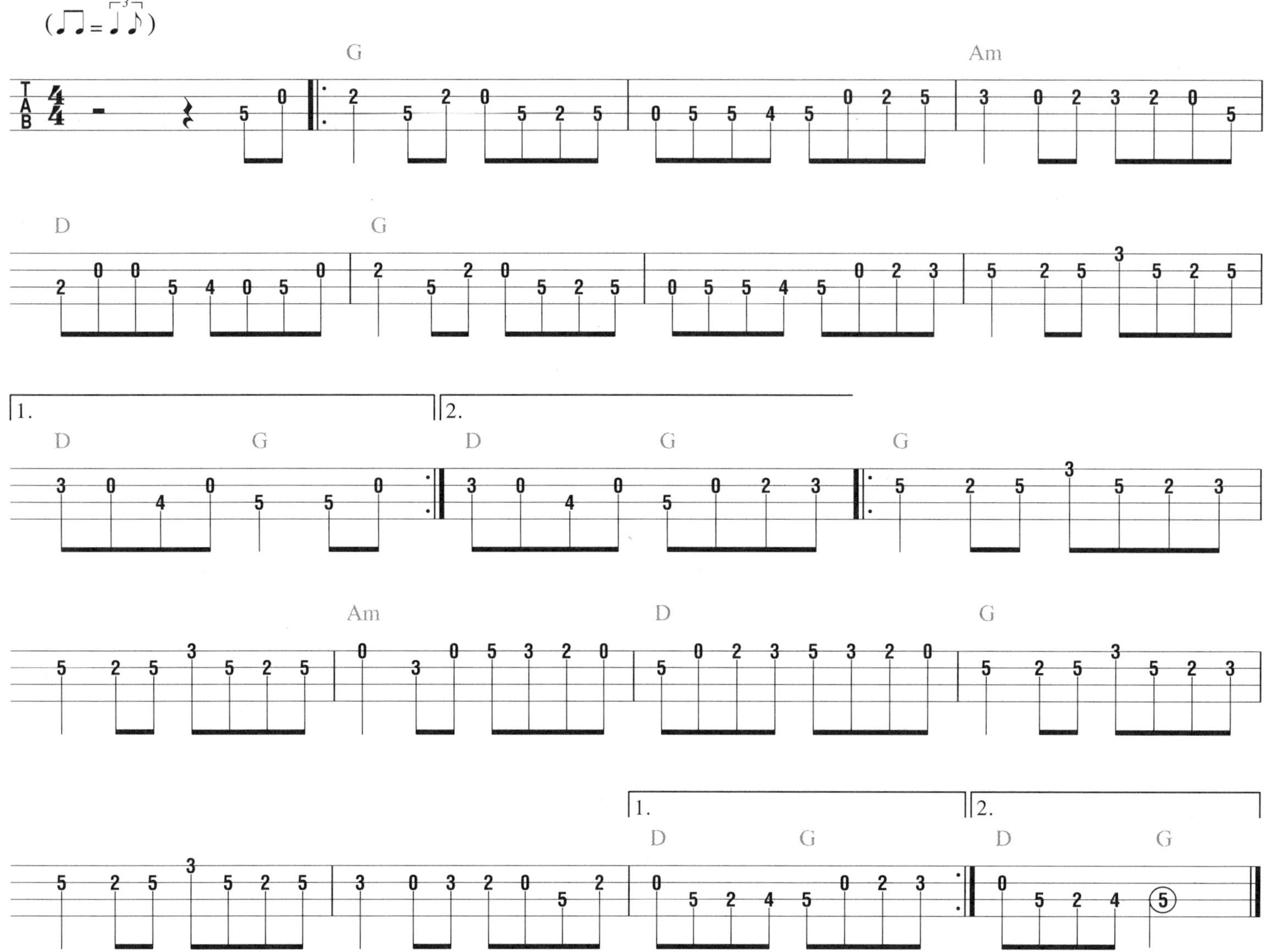

6/8 Time

A common time signature used in Celtic music is *6/8 time*. As indicated by the number on top, there are six beats per measure, and each beat is equal in length to one eighth note, according to the number on the bottom. You can count the beats as "**1**, 2, 3, 4, 5, 6" or as "**1**, 2, 3, **1**, 2, 3." I prefer the second count, because a lot of the time when we're playing a song, we'll naturally be putting the most emphasis on both of those "1" counts.

When we were playing over 4/4 and 3/4, we consistently alternated our fret-hand direction (down, up, down, up...). This worked fine in these time signatures because our eighth notes were grouped in pairs. Now, if we're counting "**1**, 2, 3, **1**, 2, 3..." for 6/8, and since the eighth notes are grouped in threes, not pairs, we can play a downstroke on the odd numbers and an upstroke on the even one (**1**, 2, 3, **1**, 2, 3 = down, up, down, down, up, down). The tricky part is that we need to play two downstrokes in a row between each 3 and 1 count.

The next two Celtic tunes are in 6/8. When using this time signature, we commonly see a new type of note used, the *dotted quarter note*. This note looks like a quarter note with a dot attached to it, and it's worth a beat and a half. (In 6/8, it can be best to think of this as equal to three eighth notes; it fills half a measure). The first rest you see in both of the following pieces is called a *dotted quarter rest*, which is equal in length to a dotted quarter note, and it tells you that nothing is played for the length of three eighth notes.

THE IRISH WASHERWOMAN

Irish Folksong

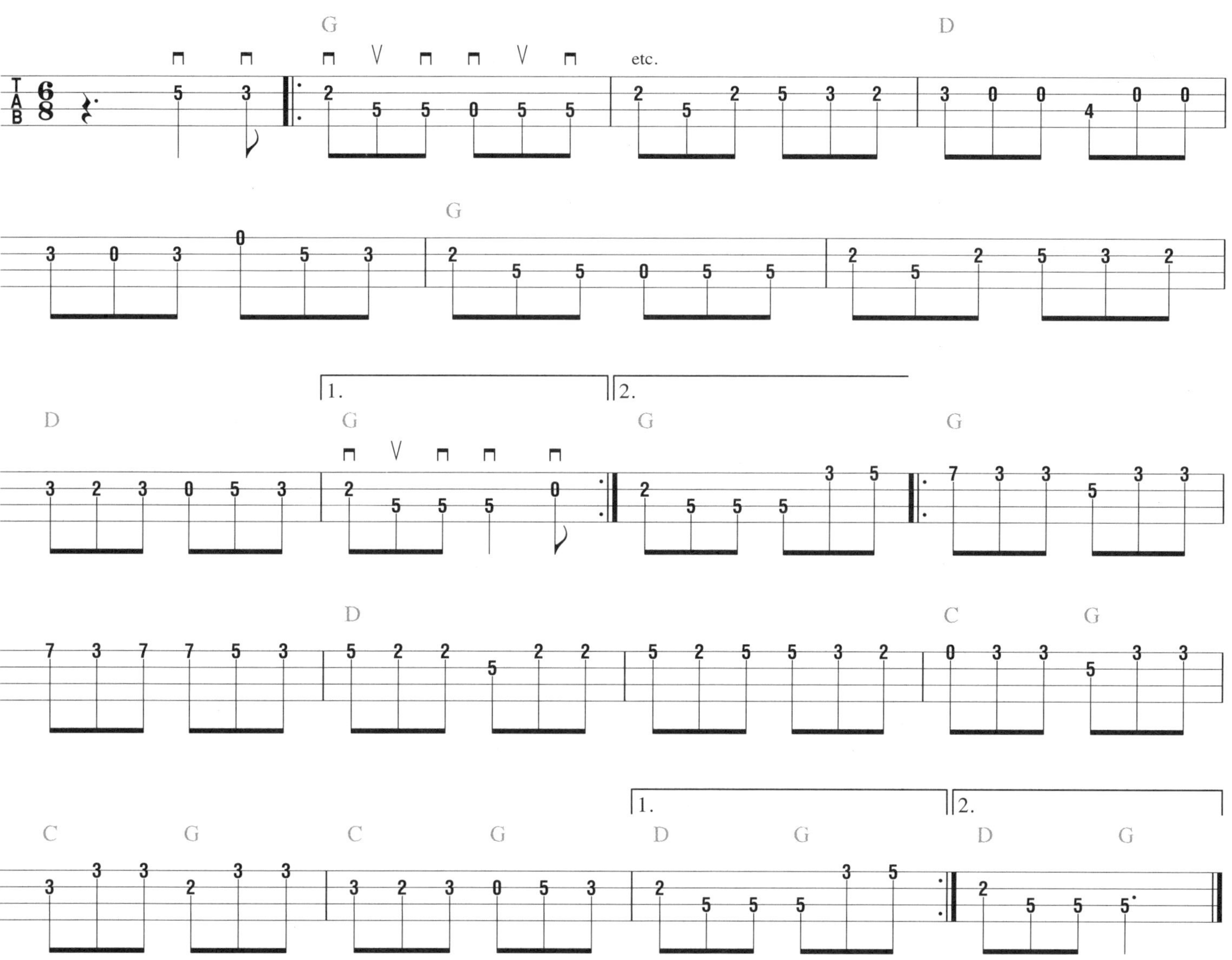

SWALLOWTAIL JIG

Traditional Irish Jig

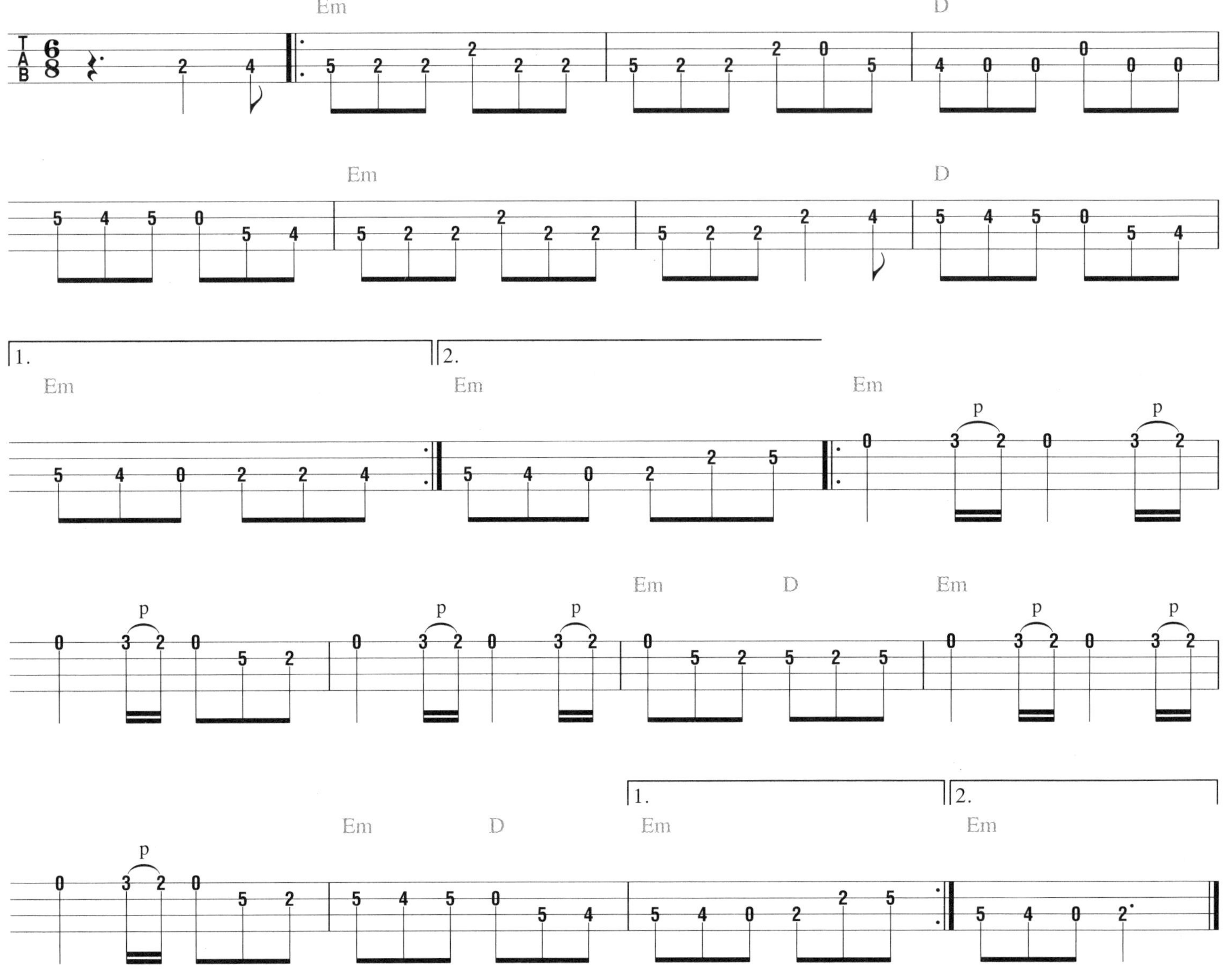

Chapter 14: Traditional Gospel

Bluegrass music not only borrows from Celtic music, but it also incorporates a wealth of traditional gospel music and hymns. Many of the familiar gospel melodies sung in churches and on bluegrass festival stages are beautifully suited for playing on the mandolin, thanks to its tuning and tonal range.

In the first song, we'll encounter a dotted quarter note in a song that uses a 4/4 time signature. Even though we're using it along with a different time signature, it's still worth one and a half beats.

PASS ME NOT O GENTLE SAVIOR

Open Position – Key of G

Words by Fanny Crosby

Music by William H. Doane

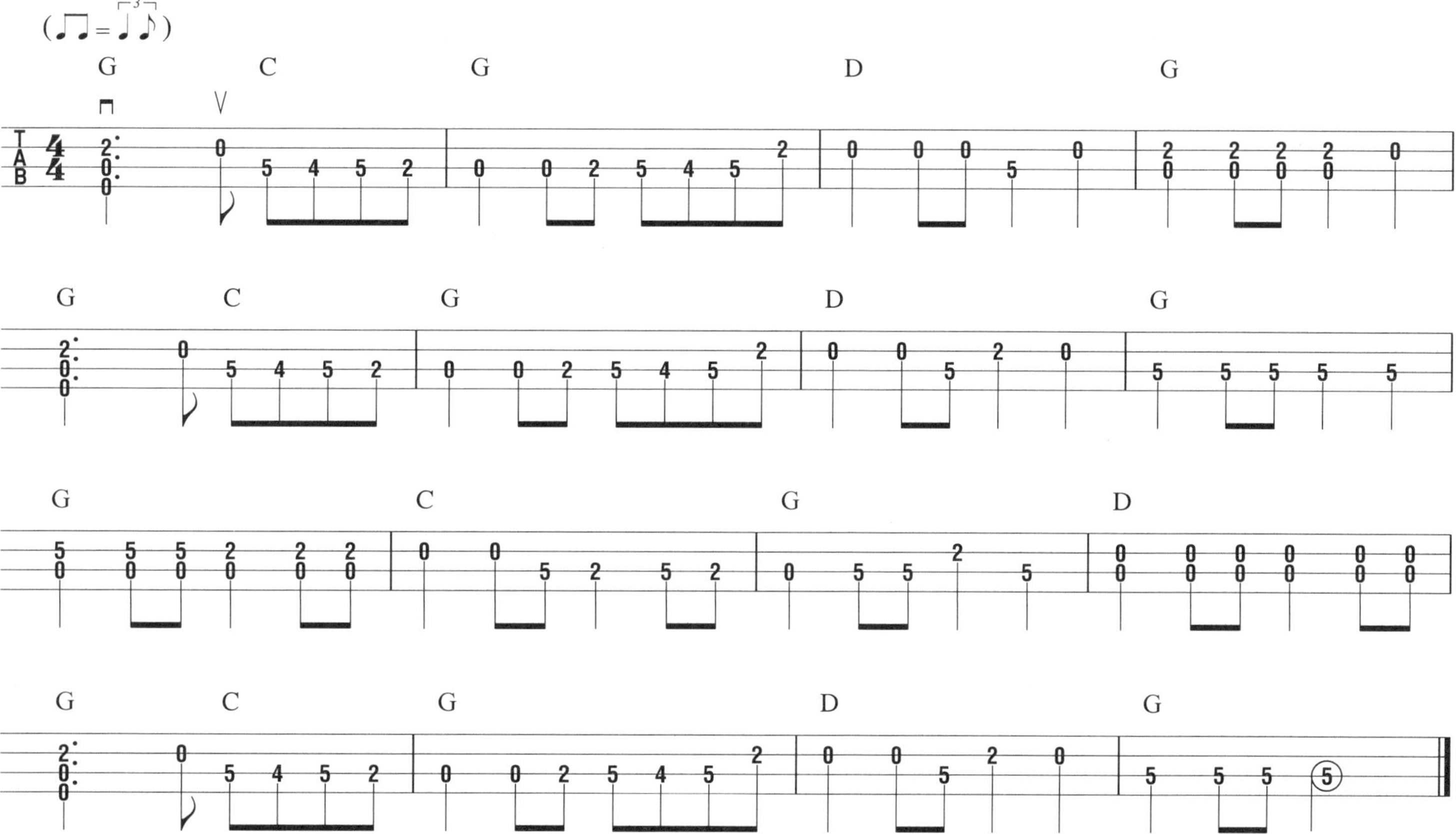

IN THE SWEET BY AND BY

Closed Position – Key of D

Words by Sanford F. Bennett
Music by Joseph P. Webster

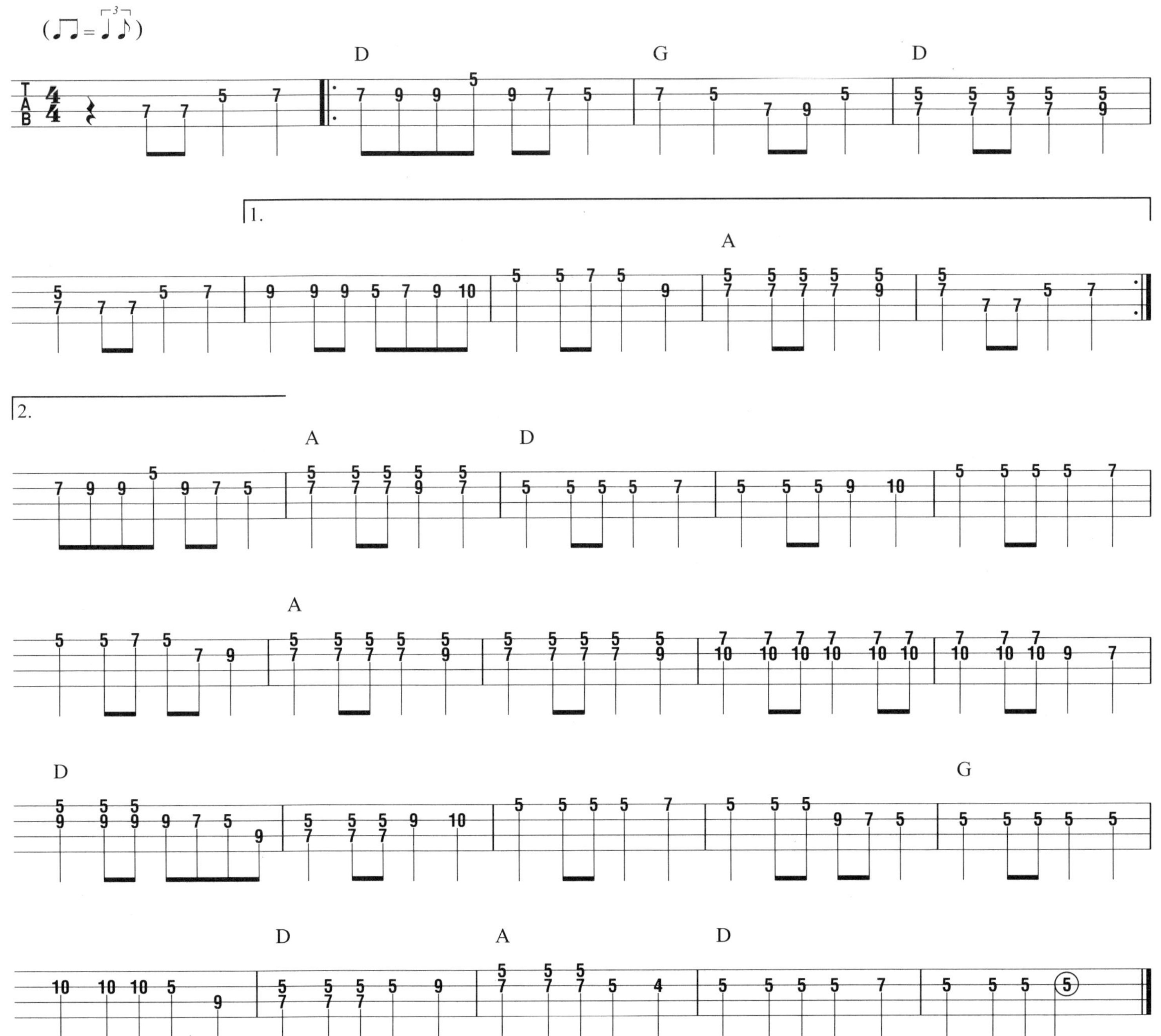

ARE YOU WASHED IN THE BLOOD?

Closed Position – Key of G

Words and Music by Elisha A. Hoffman

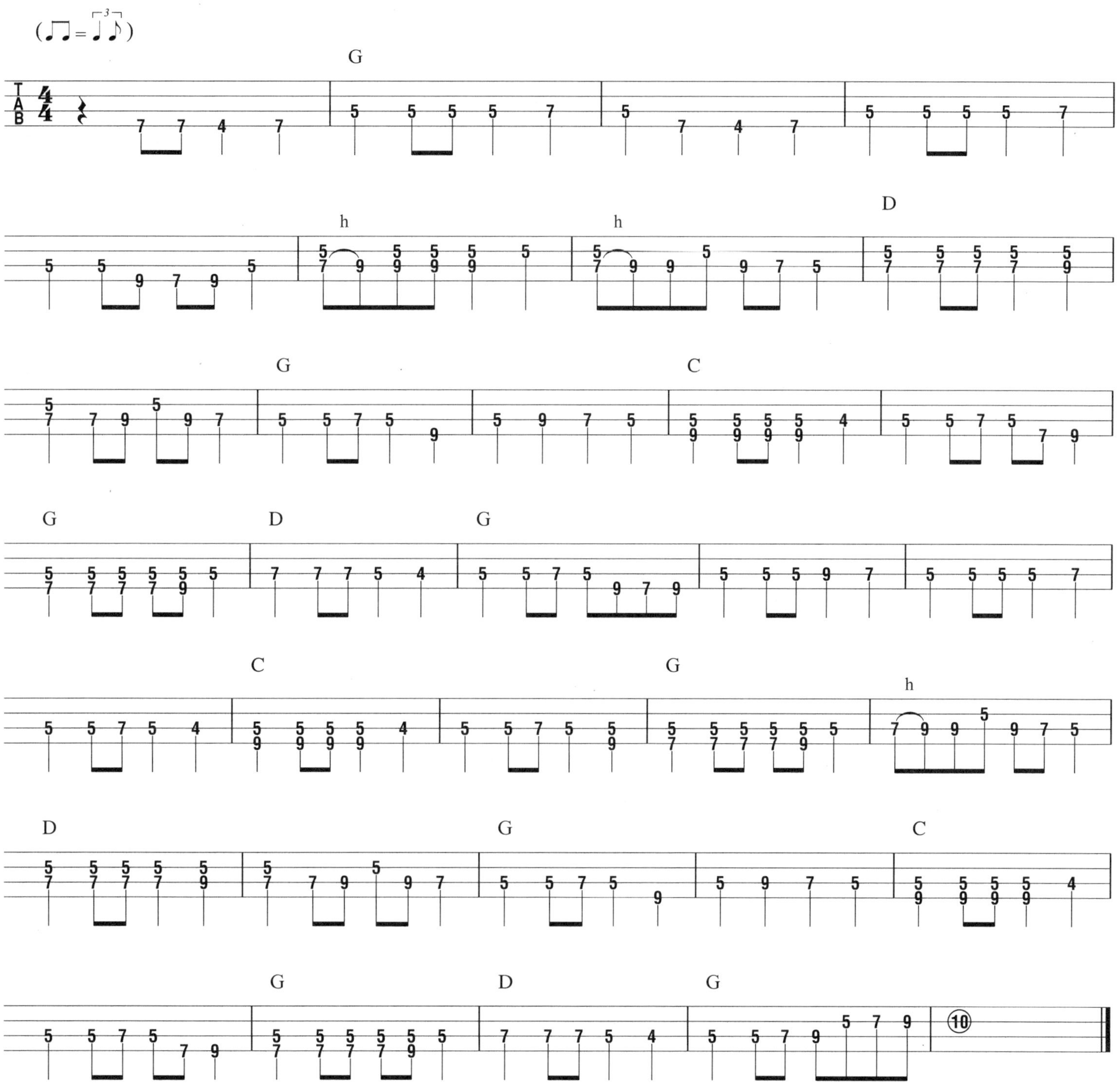

Final Thoughts

I hope you've picked up a good foundation for playing the mandolin by following along with this book. It is in no way an exhaustive course, but it should set you up well to continue exploring new songs, techniques, and ideas as you continue your journey.

Playing and teaching the mandolin has been a huge part of my life, bringing me immense joy and countless friendships. Whether you intend to play just for yourself or your goal is to perform with others, there is no end to where you can take yourself musically. Just remain patient and keep working at it. I've found that musical growth comes in spurts—you'll make great strides, hit plateaus and feel stuck for a while, and then suddenly break through to new levels. New skills just seem to emerge. Stick with it, and I'm confident you'll succeed!

Appendix A: Note Values

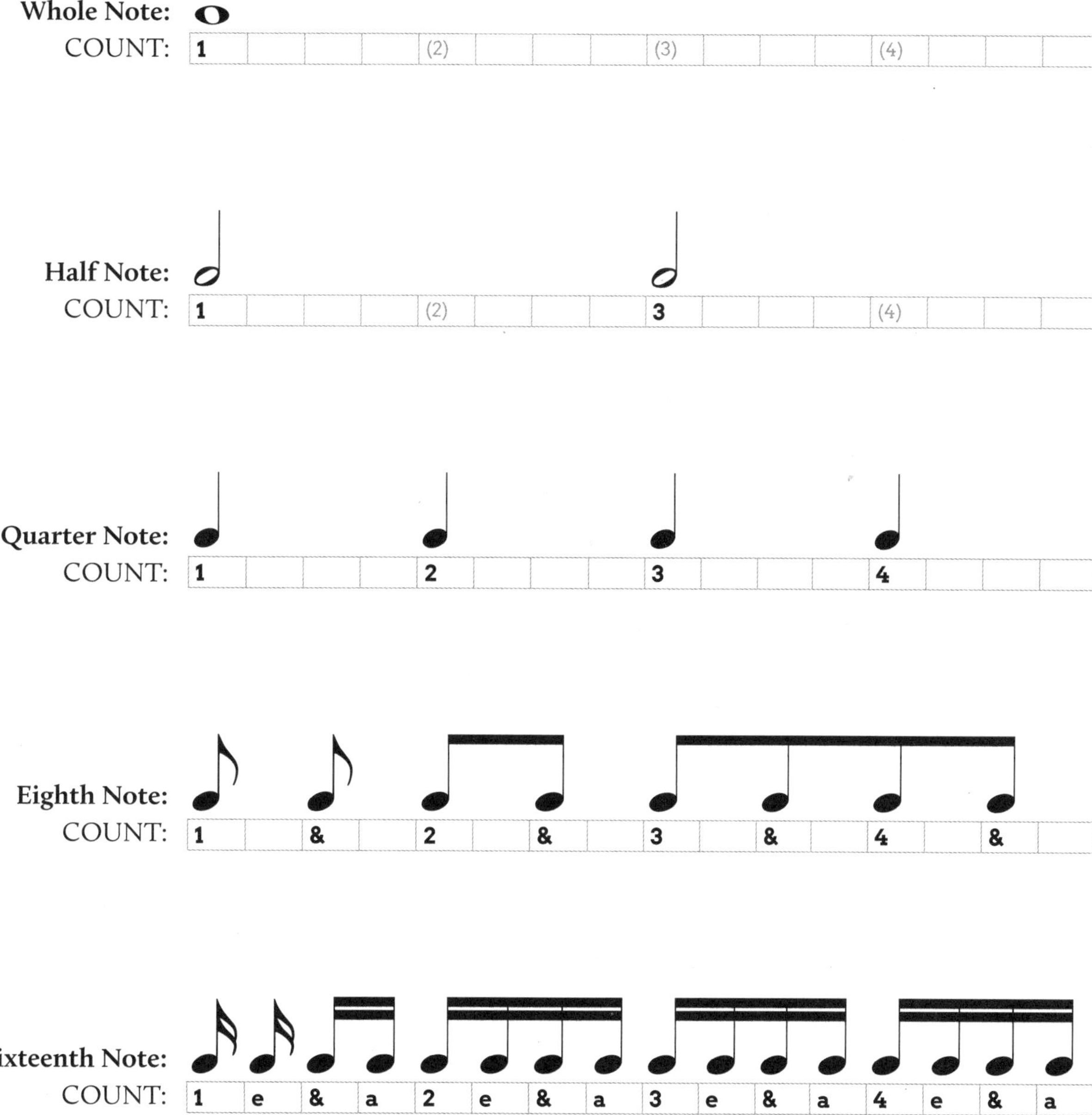

Appendix B: Note Finder

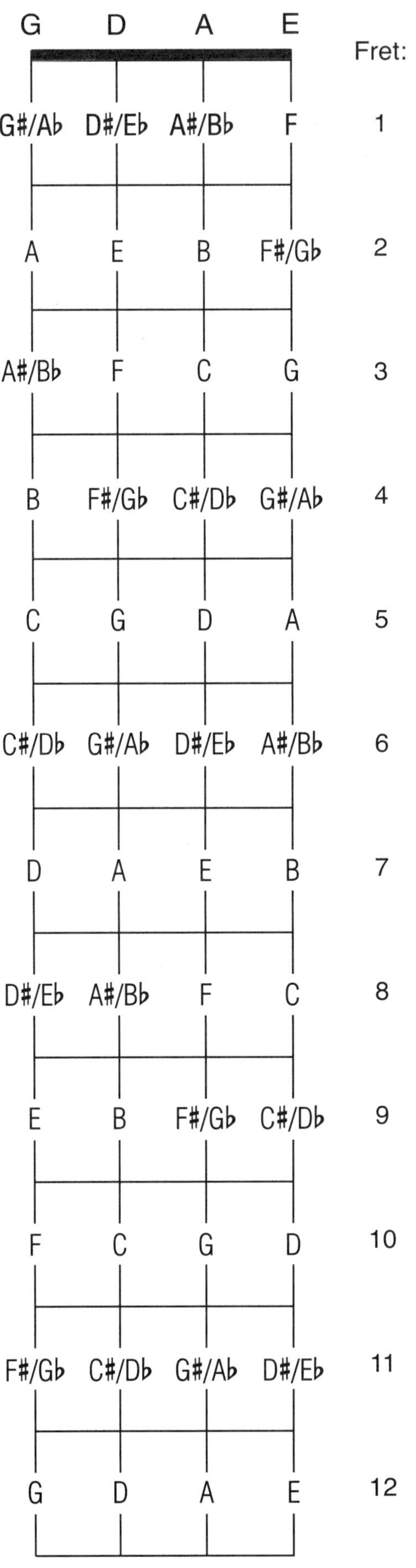

Appendix C: Chords

For more chords, check out *Mandolin Chord Finder* by Chad Johnson, available from Hal Leonard.

Open Chords

Major

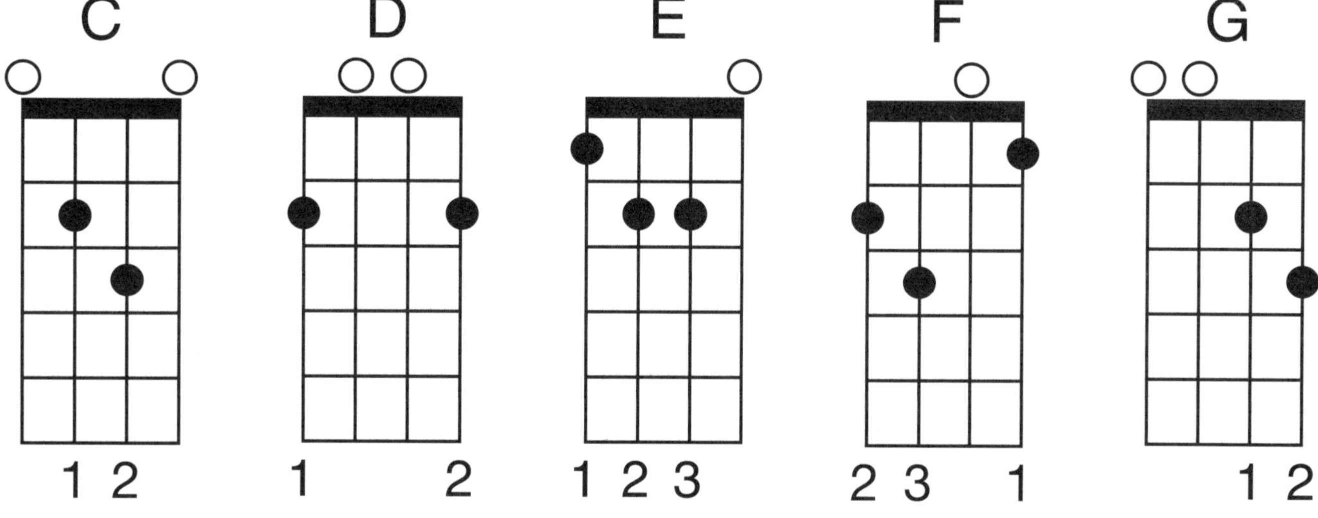

Dominant 7

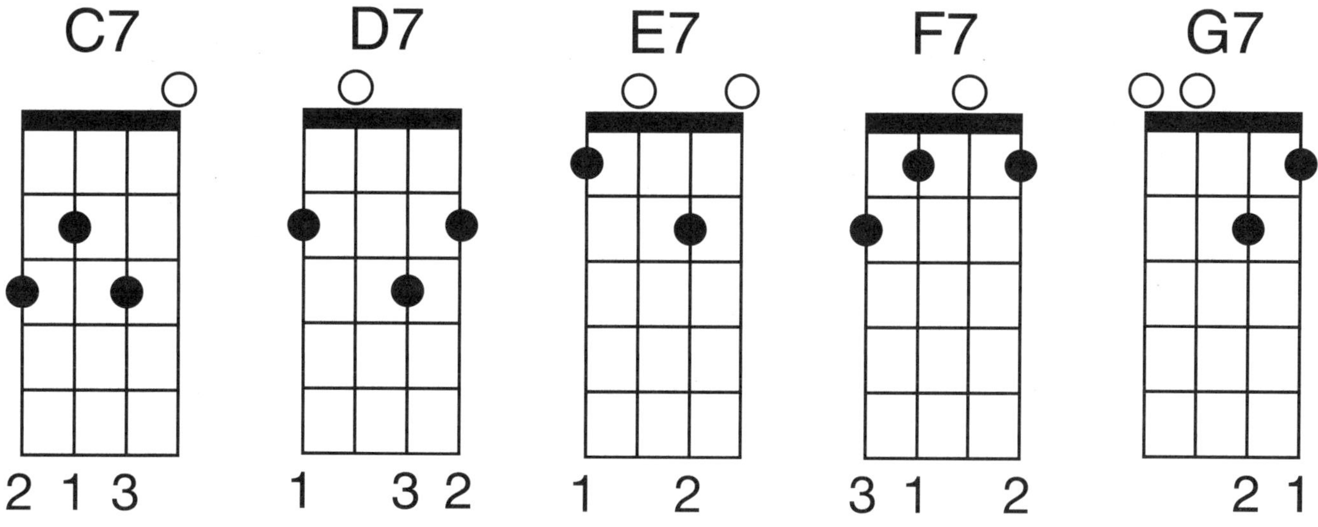

Two-Finger Chop Chords

To find sharp and flat chords, move the chord shape you already know up one fret for a sharp chord, and down one fret for a flat chord. For example, moving the G chord up one fret gives you a G♯, and moving it down one fret gives you a G♭.

Major

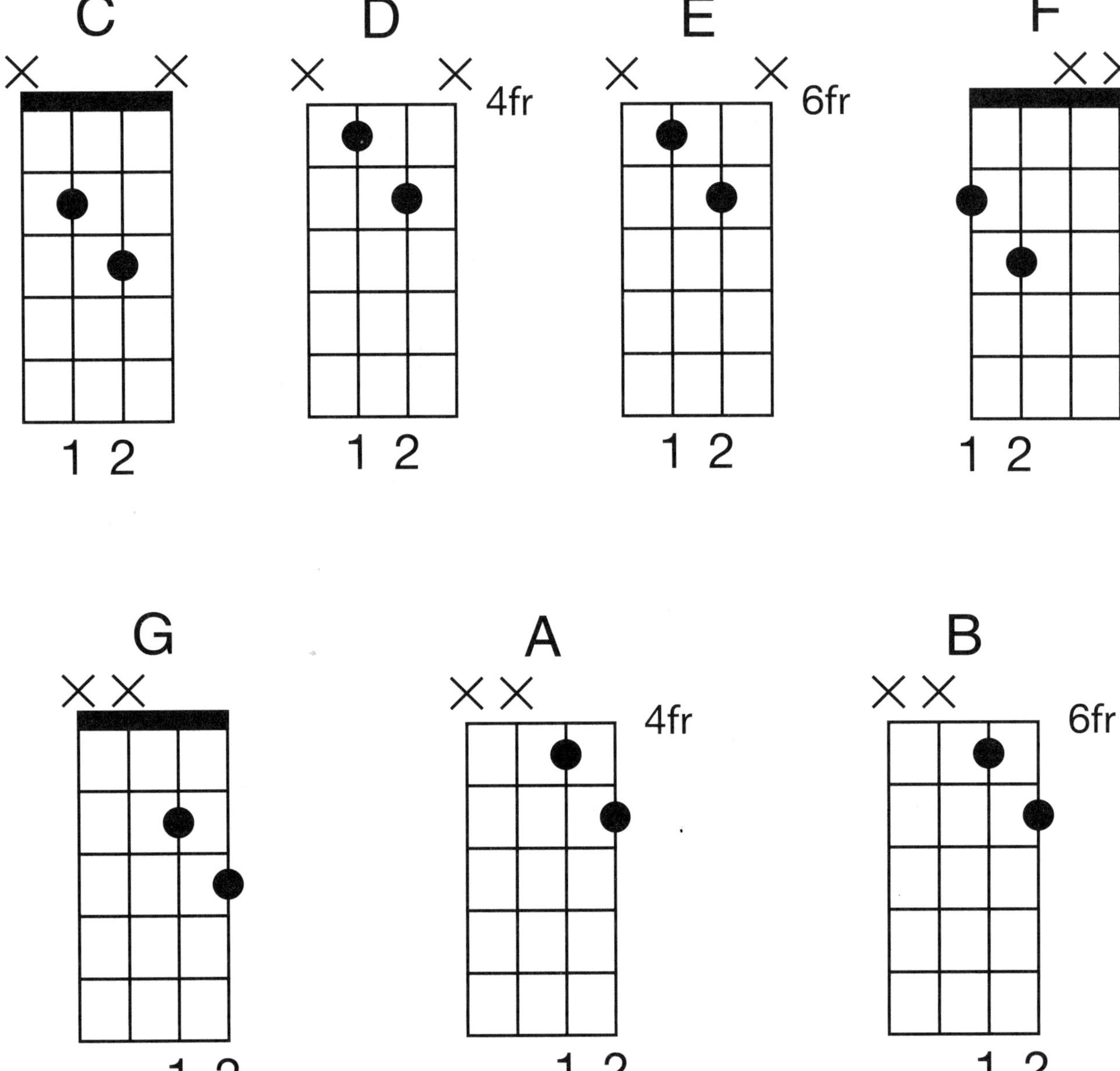

Minor

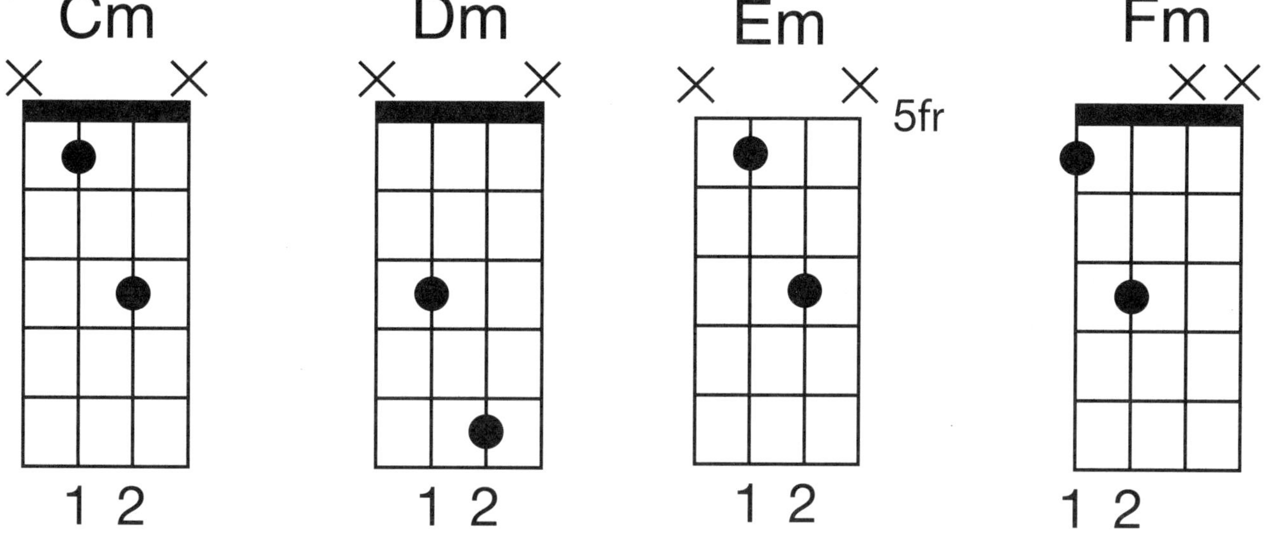

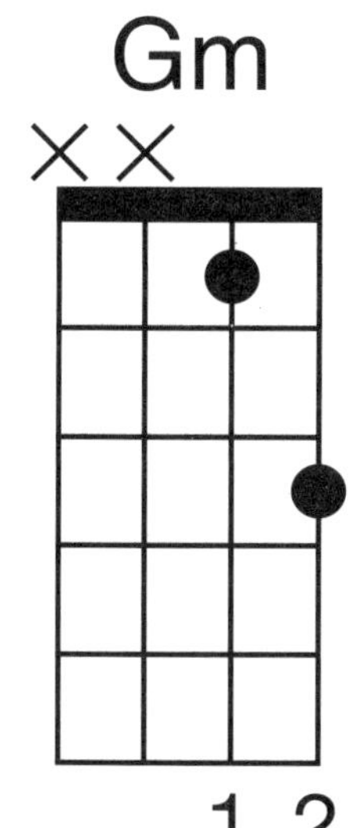

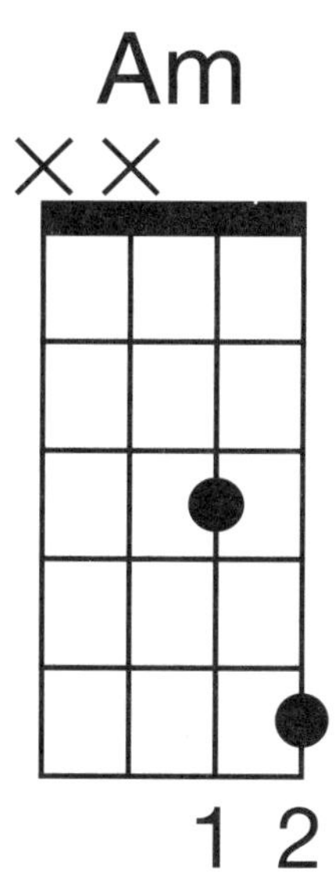

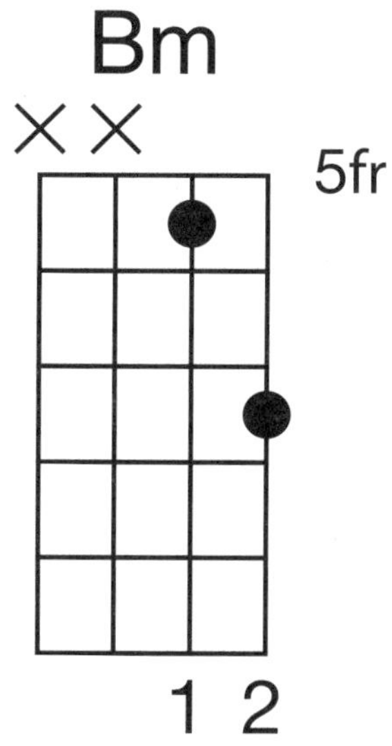

Three-Finger Chop Chords

To find sharp and flat chords, move the chord shape you already know up one fret for a sharp chord, and down one fret for a flat chord. For example, moving the G chord up one fret gives you a G♯, and moving it down one fret gives you a G♭.

Major

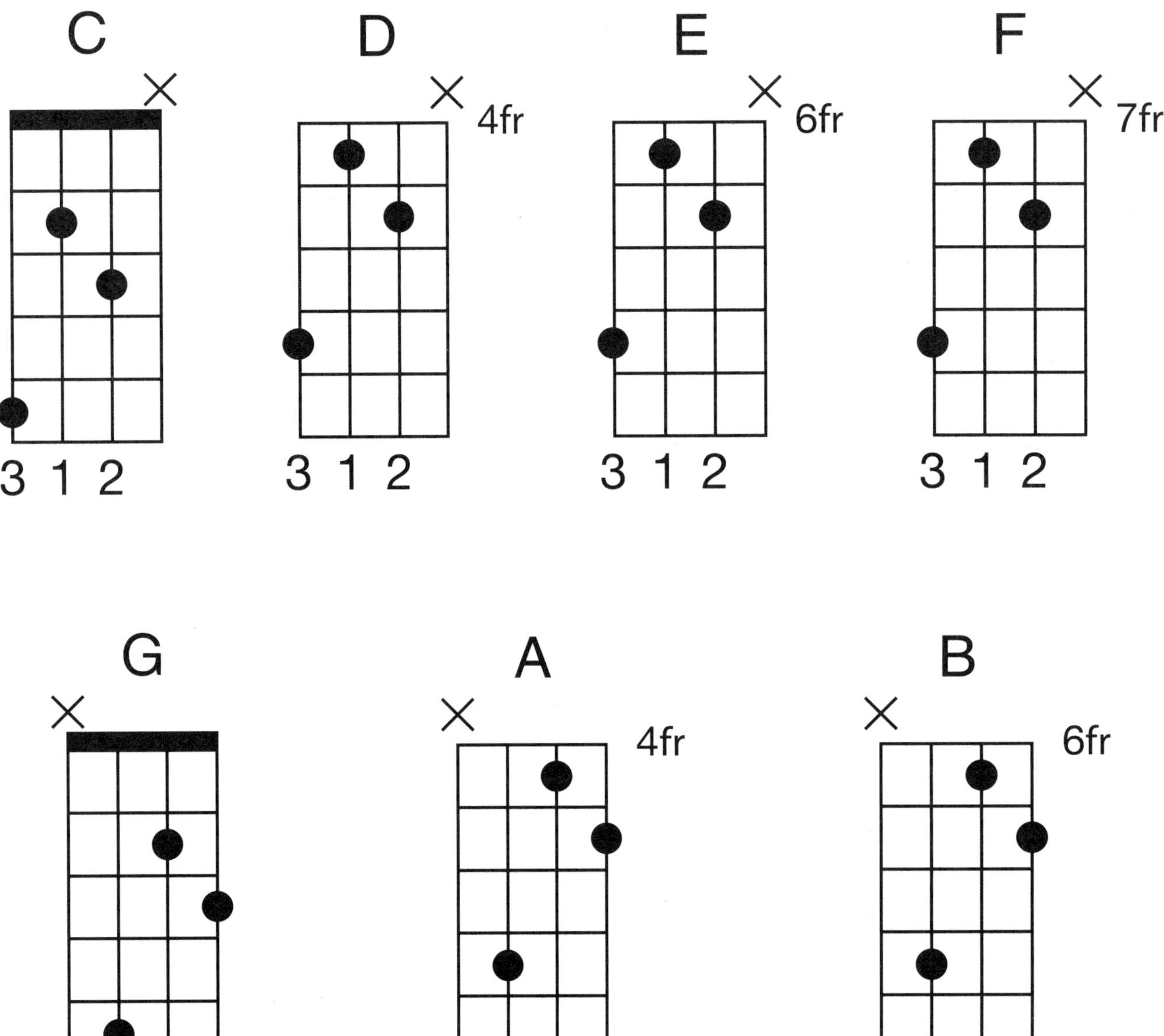

Minor

Cm
3 1 2
Dm
3fr
3 1 2
Em
5fr
3 1 2
Fm
6fr
3 1 2

Gm
3 1 2

Am
3fr
3 1 2

Bm
5fr
3 1 2

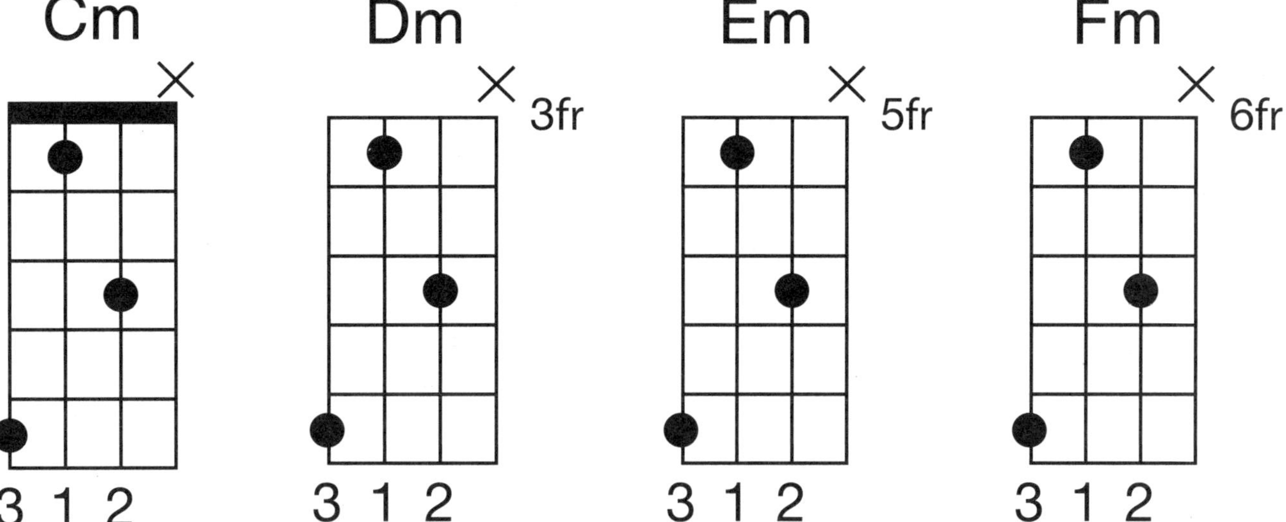

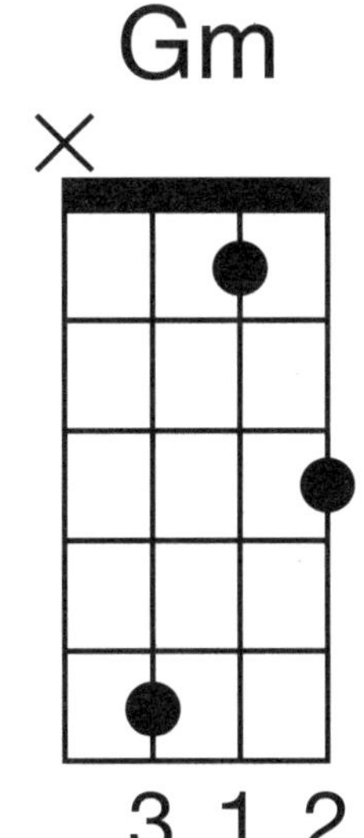

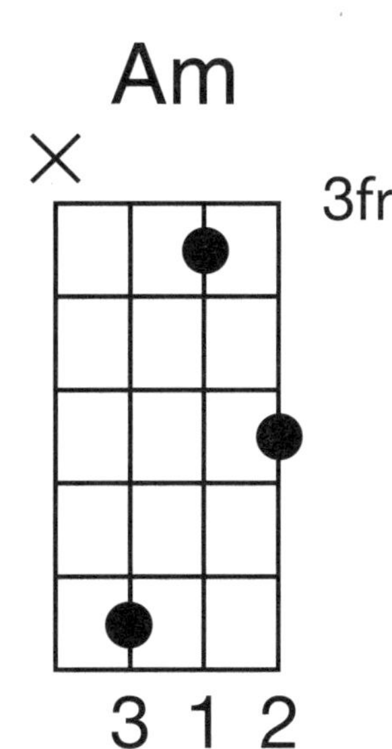

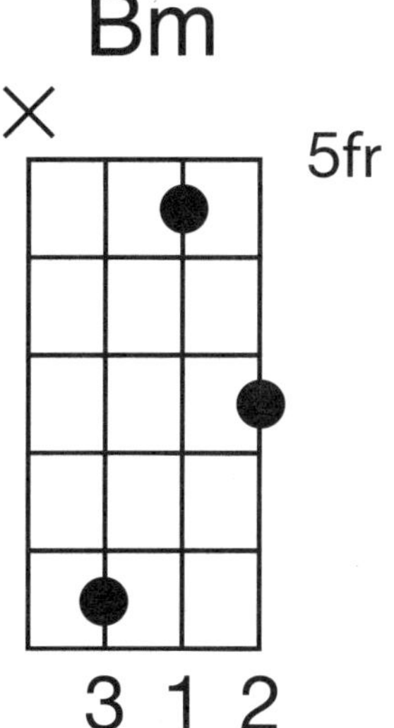

Four-Finger Chop Chords

To find sharp and flat chords, move the chord shape you already know up one fret for a sharp chord, and down one fret for a flat chord. For example, moving the G chord up one fret gives you a G♯, and moving it down one fret gives you a G♭.

Major

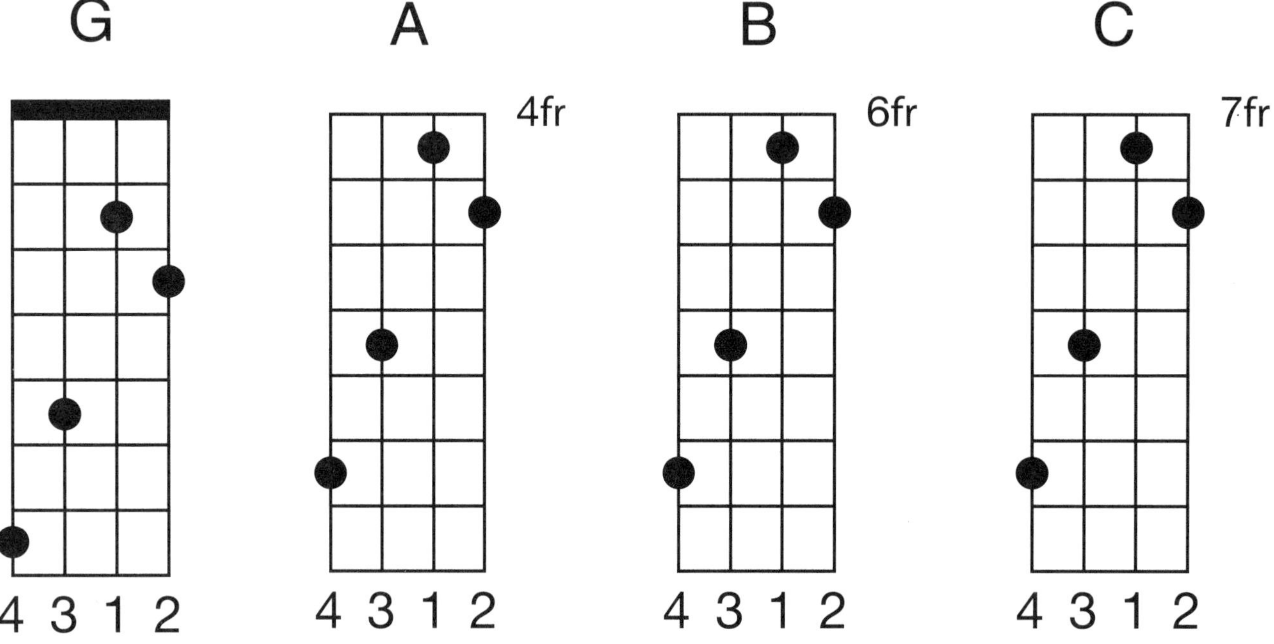

Minor

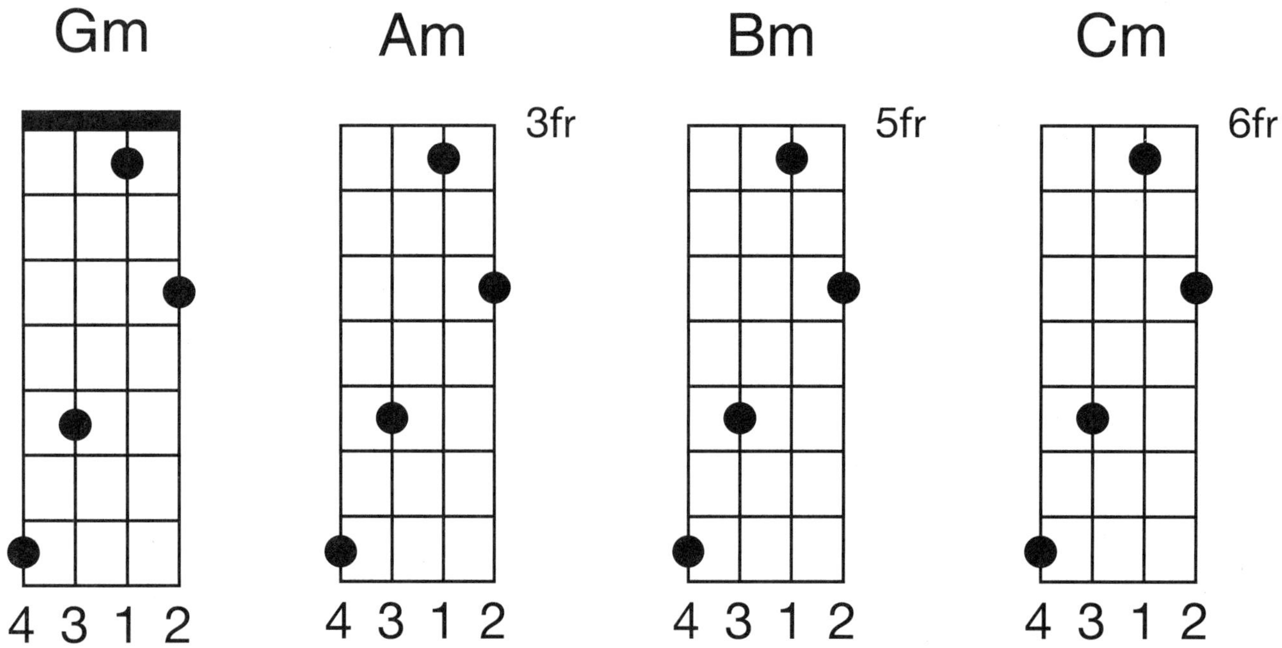

Barre Chords

To find sharp and flat chords, move the chord shape you already know up one fret for a sharp chord, and down one fret for a flat chord. For example, moving the G chord up one fret gives you a G♯, and moving it down one fret gives you a G♭. The chords used in some of the songs in this book are offered as examples of the more complicated barre chords that aren't simply major or minor.

Major

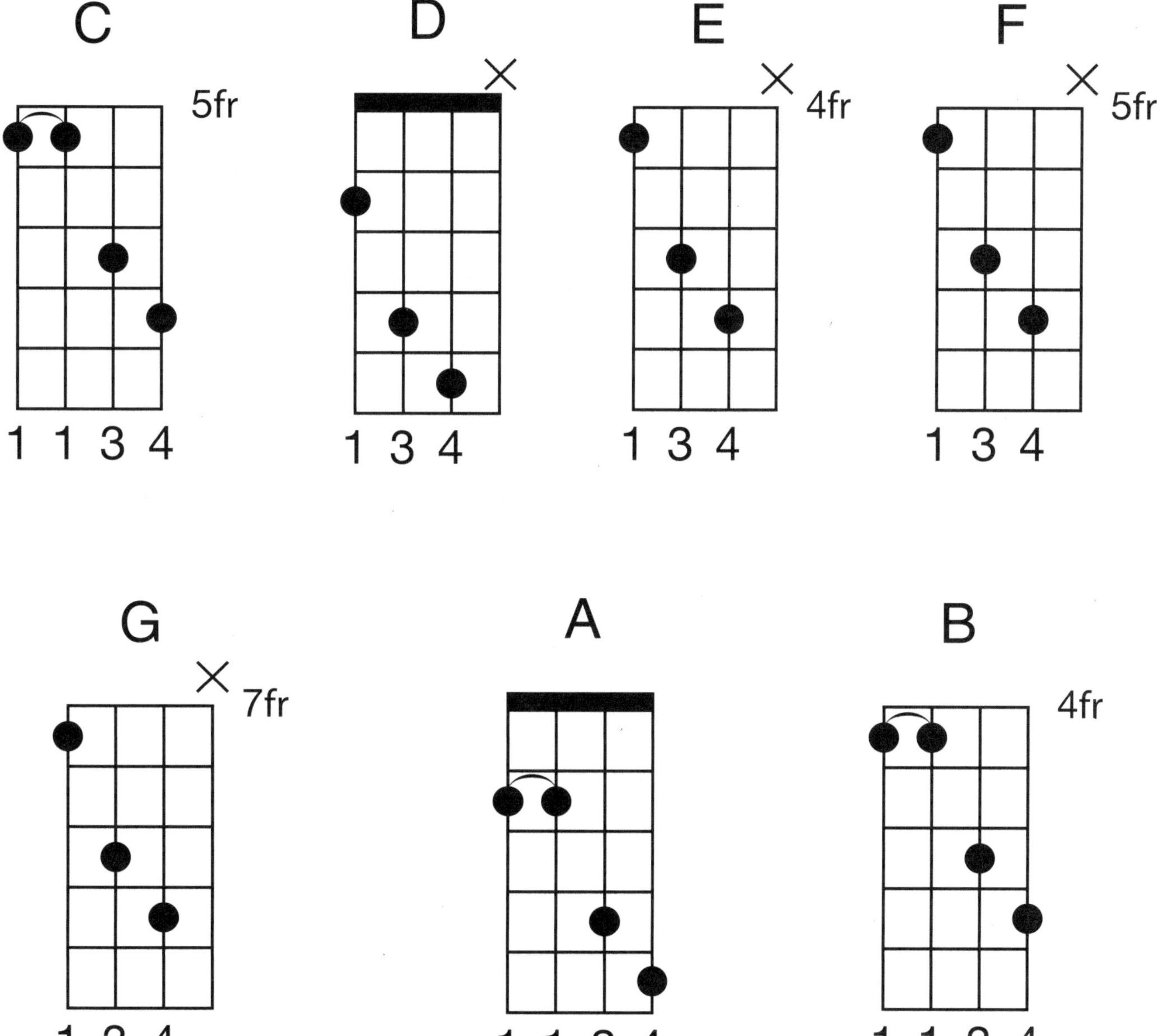

Minor

Cm
5fr
1 1 2 4
Dm
1 2 4
Em
4fr
1 2 4
Fm
5fr
1 2 4
Gm
7fr
1 2 4
Am
1 1 2 4
Bm
4fr
1 1 2 4

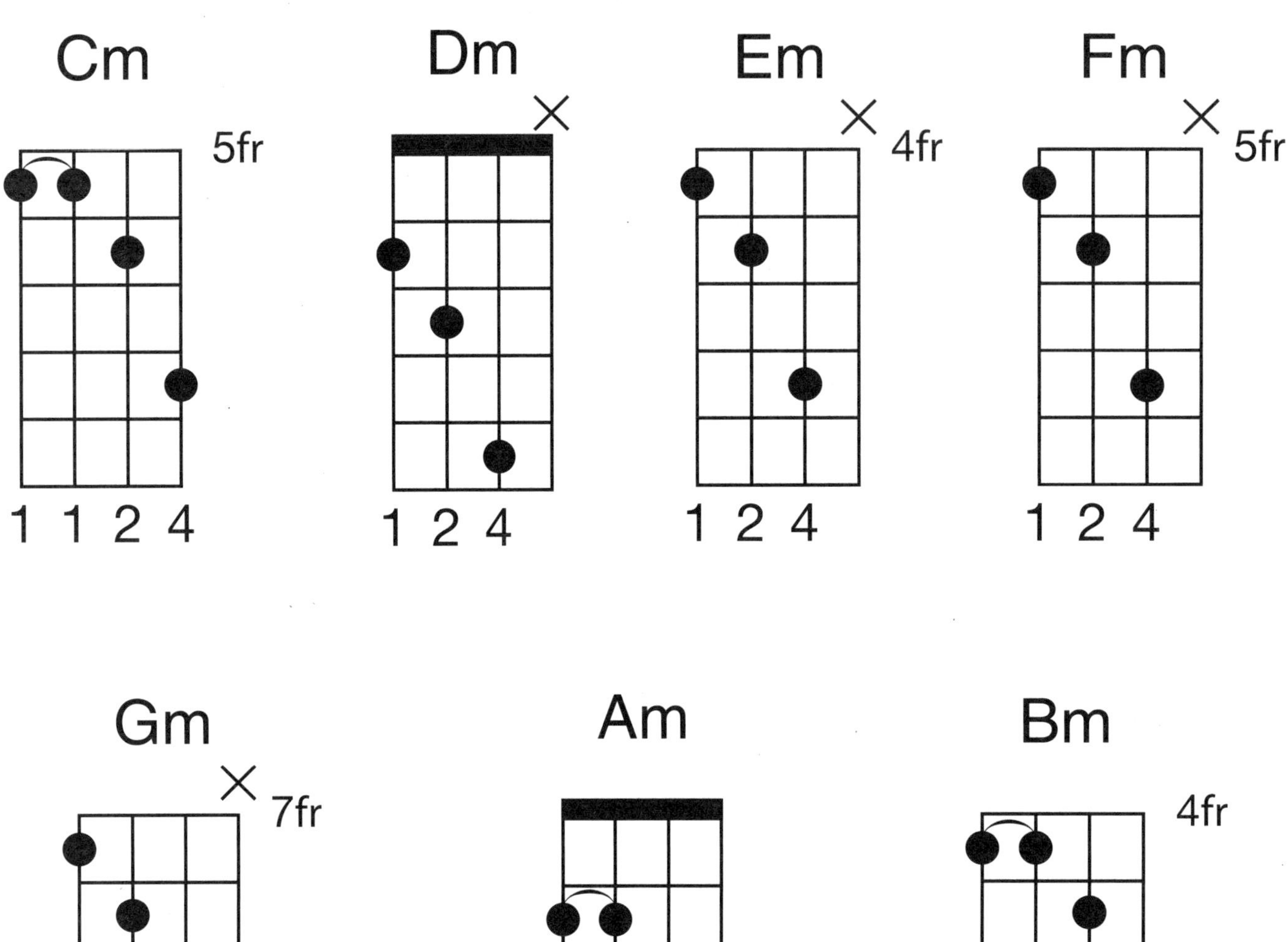

Major 7

Dmaj7

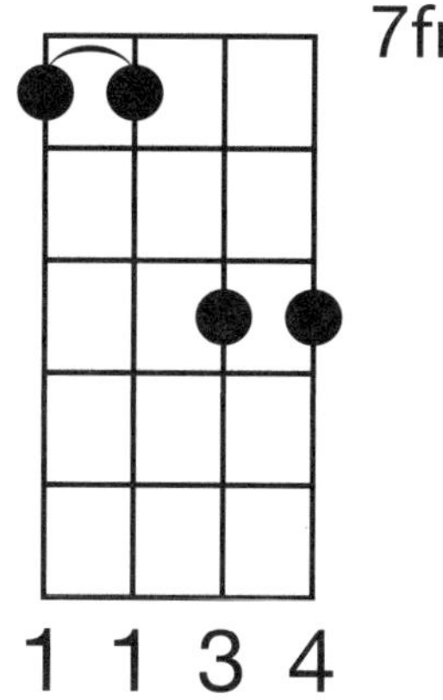

Amaj7

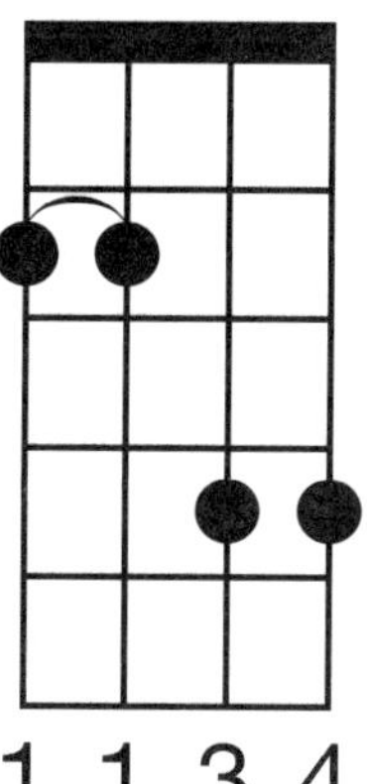

Minor (Major 7)

Em(maj7)

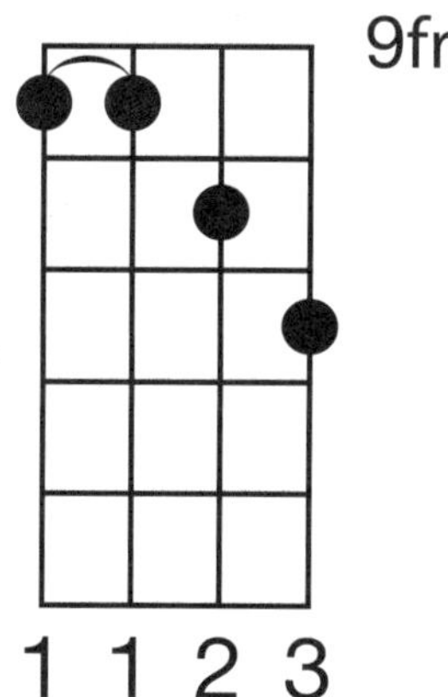

Am(maj7)

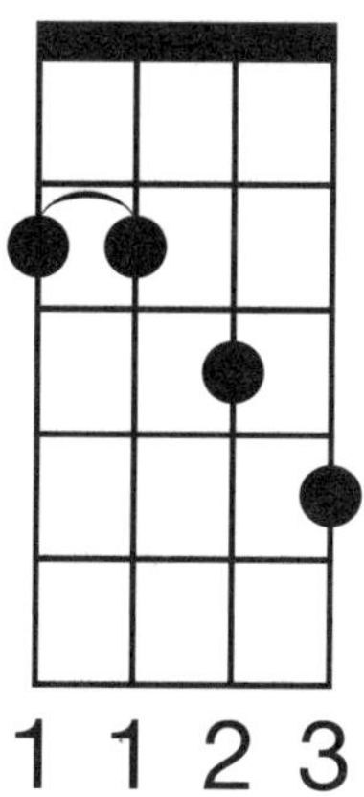

Dominant 7

C7

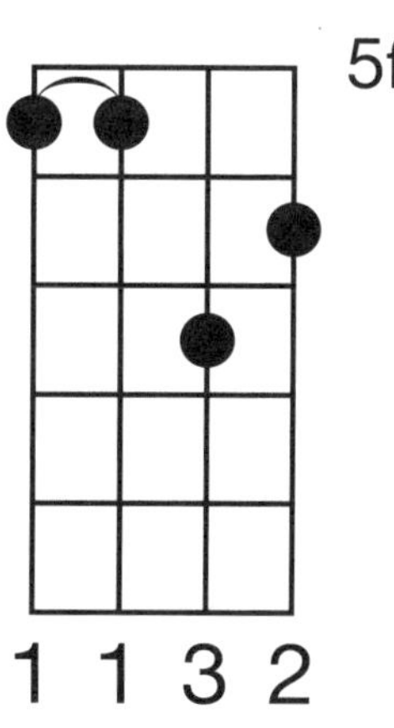

D7

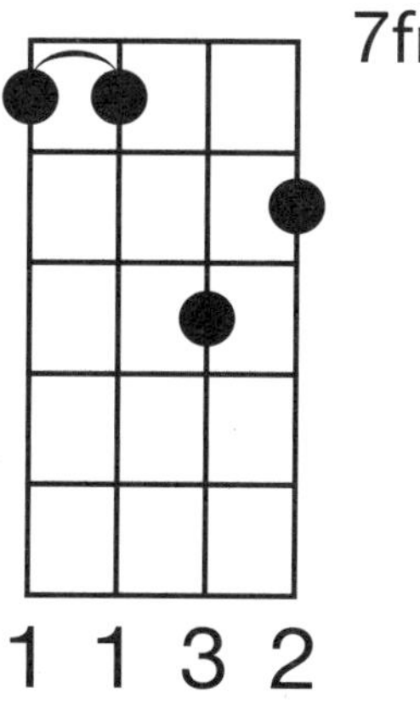

E7

A7

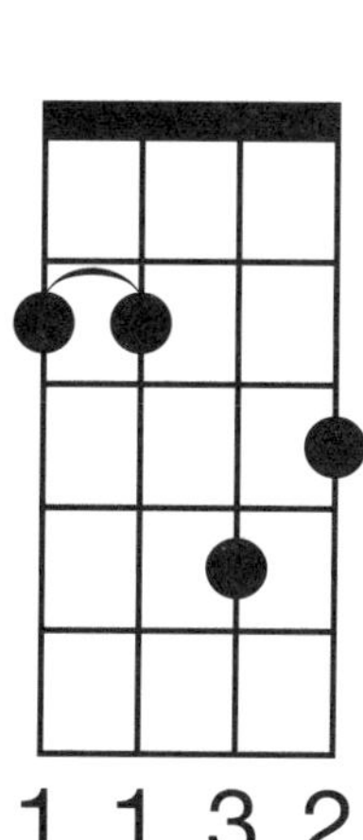

Minor 7

Am7

1 1 2 3

Major 6

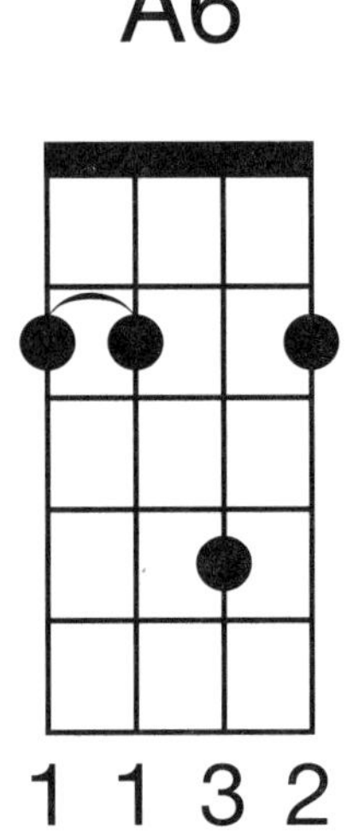

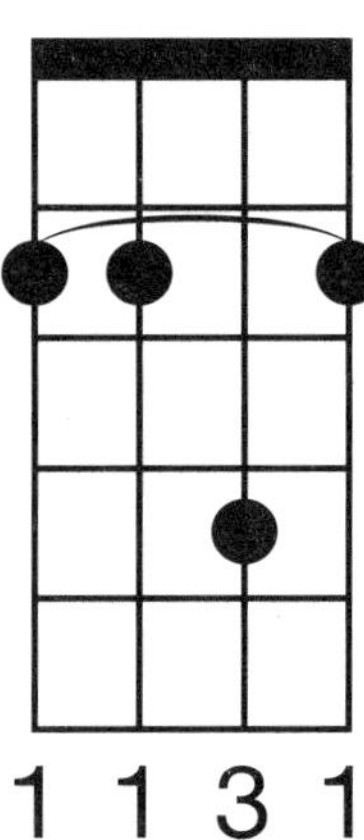

Minor 6

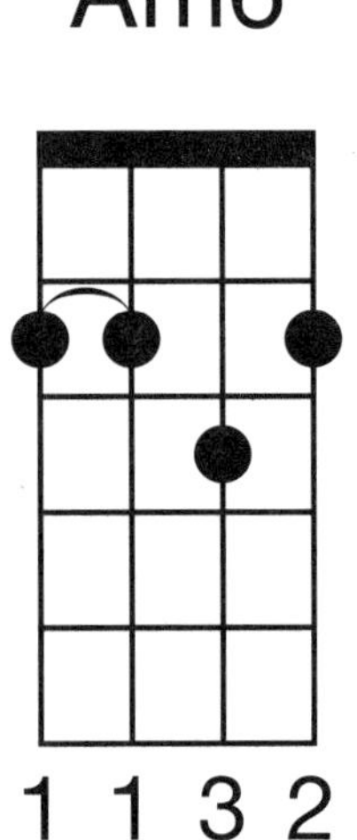

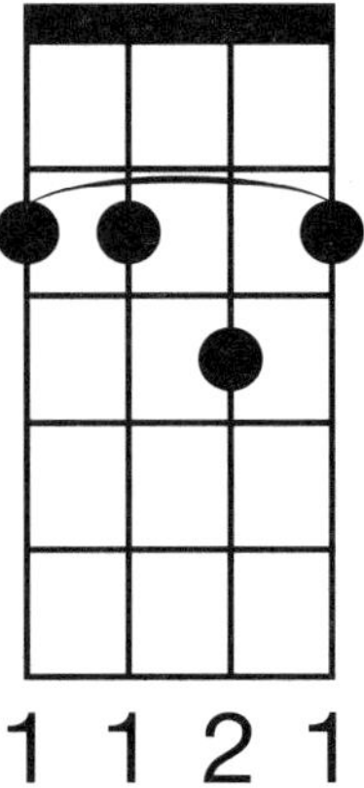